Quilting to Soothe the Soul:

Create memories for today, tomorrow, & forever

"The Beat Goes On," by Ricky Tims, Arvada, Colorado.

Linda Carlson

Published by

 **krause publications**
An F&W Publications Company

700 East State Street • Iola, WI 54990-0001
715-445-2214 • 888-457-2873
www.krause.com

Please call or write for our free catalog of publications. To place an order or obtain a free catalog, please call 800-258-0929. For editorial comment, please use our regular business telephone 715-445-2214.

Library of Congress Catalog Number 2002113126
ISBN 0-87349-541-1

Table of Contents

Dedication

To my youngest daughter Meredith, the talented photographer:
Whether we shoot a photo or pick up a needle,
May we always find solace in each other and in
The labor of our hands to express the joys and sorrows in
our hearts.

I also want to thank my daughter Amy Carlson Nord for acting as
ex-officio editor-in-residence while recuperating from
giving us our first grandchild, Emma Kate. Her computer
formatting knowledge was invaluable!

"Patchwork? Ah, no! It was memory, imagination, history, biography, joy, sorrow, philosophy, religion, romance, realism, life, love, and death; and over all, like a halo, the love of the artist for his work and the soul's longing for earthly immortality."

Eliza Calvert Hall
Aunt Jane of Kentucky (1907)

"What with rearin' a family, and tendin' to a home, and all my chores — that quilt was a long time in the frame. The story of my life is pieced into it. All my joys and all my sorrows."

Lincoln County, West Virginia, Quilter
The Mountain Artisans Quilting Book (1973)

Introduction

The Labor of Your Hands Works Through the Anxiety and Grief in Your Heart

"I stitched to soothe my sorry soul" is a phrase that has been uttered by many quilters when they needed to occupy their hectic minds and nervous hands with the smooth, gentle, rhythmic, and repetitive motions of quilting. The reason for the need to stitch doesn't matter, but the cathartic movement of hand sewing and quilting is the cure. After interviewing many quilters, I have found that grief experiences do not always involve losing loved ones to death. Indeed, ended marriages, children leaving home for new horizons, and family or friends moving across the country were reasons to begin a special quilting project to commemorate the event as well as provide a sense of closure for the quiltmaker.

The initial reason for writing this book began back in the late 1980s, when I was first attracted to four-block quilts because of their big, bold, beautiful patterns. I thought, "These were meant for me to make. I won't live long enough to make all the wonderful patterns I see in magazines, books, calendars, and Show & Tell at guild meetings—and these have only four blocks!"

In 1993, just as I was joyously celebrating receiving a contract from the American Quilter's Society for my first book, *Roots, Feathers & Blooms: 4-Block Quilts Their History & Patterns*, my world was shattered by the sudden death of my wonderful father. I can distinctly recall how his face beamed with pride when he read my dedication page, which in part read ... "To my dad, Frederick Herman Giesler, who was always the first to say, 'We're proud of all you kids'".... In the wake of my grief, I instinctively turned to quilting to soothe my sorry soul. I was working on the trapunto weeping willow border of "Meredith's Tree of Life at Midnight" (which appears on the cover of this book) for my younger daughter when he died, and suddenly the tree's symbolic lore of grief and sadness became all too real for me. I could sit, stitch, and sob through this grief journey as my ancestors had done before me with their mourning and memorial or casket quilts.

Months passed, and I started collecting data about these quilts in anticipation of being able to reach out to other quilters who were facing difficult situations and needed a cathartic project to occupy their hands and ease their hearts. During this research process, I developed six initial 15-inch wide by 45-inch long commemorative, memorial or casket quilt patterns to share with all quilters, including those who just wanted some control over their own funerary arrangements. If you want to use them as casket covers, they are designed to lie over the bottom half of the casket with ample room for the traditional floral spray.

In the year 2000, I gave lectures about the historic and current role of quilts in the grieving process, and received extremely enthusiastic responses. One student who took the accompanying three-hour workshop to make one of these quilts later brought her mother to my home and said, "Mom, this is something I want to do for you before the time comes. I want you to pick out the pattern so I'll know you'll like it." Her mother was so moved that her daughter wanted to do this for her as a special good-bye testament to their love and respect for one another. What makes this story even more poignant is the fact that the daughter is a cancer survivor.

General Information and Supplies

The patterns and quilting motifs can be duplicated exactly, or you may mix and match the designs to suit individual tastes and skills. All the appliqué techniques are suitable for beginners as well as those who are more advanced. The quilting designs are suitable for all. Some of the elegantly simple designs can be made in three days, while the more intricate designs may require more time. Prewash all fabrics to prevent later shrinkage.

General supplies include paper and fabric scissors, fabric markers, ruler, compass, freezer paper or template plastic, pins, needles, matching threads for appliqué motifs, quilting threads, and the quiltmaker's choice of batting. I prefer Hobbs wool batting because of its soft hand and washability. A sewing machine may be used for attaching bindings and/or for any of the pattern pieces the quiltmaker wishes to assemble by machine.

Notes From the Author

Some words of wisdom need to be examined in the positive healing light of humor such as: "Life is not a parade nor a bowl of cherries, but most of the time it sure beats the alternative." Everyone deals with stress in their lives in different ways, some of which are helpful and healthy. Making quilts is one of the healthy ways to deal with stress.

From the time I was a sophomore in high school, I've been teaching *something*. At first, it was piano lessons for $.75/hour and my students' ages ranged from six to one adult dad who reasoned that his son would have an advantage if he himself had some keyboard knowledge. Eventually, I graduated from the University of Missouri-Columbia with two teaching degrees, so it is not surprising that two of my books contain research projects. The teacher in me says students need background knowledge of a topic before they can proceed to develop their own opinions and styles—whether in music or quiltmaking. Therein lies my need to educate the reader about the historical significance and role quilts have had in dealing with grief in all its forms.

Grief and grieving today are most often—but not exclusively—associated with a loved one's dying. Grief is, by its very nature, a sensitive subject to privately or publicly discuss. Knowing that led me to research commemorative, memorial, mourning, and casket quilts.

By definition, a commemorative quilt honors an event or person whether the event was survived or not, and can be created during the event, or afterward, as a tribute. A memorial or mourning piece is usually done after a death, but can be created in anticipation, as some quiltmakers did and still do in all parts of the world. Many times a quilt in progress has become a mourning or memorial quilt by adding special symbols in the quilting or appliqué motifs such as a baby's hand, a harp or angel, a lily or cross, etc. Some symbols, as you will see, were pieced using just black and white or gray fabrics. Others were elaborately appliquéd and stitched with memorial verses and the person's vital statistics. Casket or coffin quilts were usually created before the event. Some were made to follow the shape of the coffin with the shoulder area being wider and tapering to the foot of the coffin. When funerals were held in homes, they were used to cover the body or coffin, and may have been buried with them or passed down in the family to be used in the same way again and again –making such quilts rare finds today.

Foreword

In his Palm Sunday, 2002 sermon titled "A Strange Parade," Reverend Randall Sawyer of the Mexico, Missouri Disciples of Christ Church talked about Christ's humble donkey ride to Calvary, and repeated several times: "Life is not a parade. Life is an ongoing process of dying." Here is an excerpt from that sermon that so eloquently states the need for a book of this kind in our personal libraries:

"Death is not our favorite topic of conversation. And most of us try our best to avoid it. We go through life as if it's a parade—a parade to Cub Scout meetings and dance recitals, a parade to graduations and weddings, a parade to career opportunities, and to church, and to retirement.

"But here on Palm Sunday, we come face-to-face with a troubling reality. Life is not a parade. Life is an ongoing process of dying. And what God seeks to open our eyes to is the fact that dying is not something that happens only at the end of our lives, but all through our lives! At every turn.

"The birth of a baby is a dying from the world of the womb to a cold and unfamiliar place. When a child is weaned, she's severed from the only source of comfort and nourishment she's known. When a child learns to walk, she walks away from her mother. When she leaves for school, it's the end of the security of home.

"Growing up is a process of dying. Adolescence is the death of childhood. Young adulthood is true separation from parental supervision.

"And then, there's marriage! That can be a dying! The bride and groom may see their wedding as an exuberant joy, but mom and dad sit there with tears in their eyes. There's a kind of death there. And, in fact, marriage, to some extent, is a kind of death, too. Death to privacy. Death to independence. Death to unilateral decisions. Death to the notion that there's only one way of doing things. We die to singleness, and are faced with life as a couple.

"And on and on the process goes. Dying to couplehood in order to have children. Sometimes experiencing divorce and separation. Sometimes dealing with physical death itself.

"We ask those painful questions like, 'Why do I have cancer? Why am I widowed?' As Jesus rides into the deaths of life, God exalts Him!"

When there is stress in your life of any kind, turn to your needle. Whether this little quilt is meant to be a final quilt for yourself or a loved one, or to commemorate an event in your life, the simple act of sewing and quilting it will bring your breathing and heart rate down to a normal level, and you will experience physiological and emotional peace. In this transitional journey, may you remember the good times, laughter and love, and find peace in creating this quilt.

"Tears; A Healing Quilt"

1991 by Judy B. Dales, Kingwood, Texas. Photography by The Photographic House.

Judy Dales has found that designing and stitching quilts has helped her through some of the hardest times in her life. Quilting saved her sanity when her mother was diagnosed with lung cancer. She was able to continue her handwork in preparation for classes or exhibits while traveling to Vermont to care for her mother one summer.

Several months after her mother died, Judy experienced a lack of creativity, and this was very stressful to her because she knew from twenty years of experience that handwork had always been very soothing and comforting.

Joen Wolfram contacted Judy about creating an iridescent quilt for her forthcoming book, *The Magical Effects of Color*. Judy drew abstract curve designs and chose whites, pinks, yellows, turquoises, and peaches over a background of a variety of different gray tones. These softer colors gave the quilt an opalescent aura, a form of iridescence. The curves were wavy, and as she stepped back to view them, they became droplet shapes or tears, which struck her as very appropriate. Making the quilt brought her peace, and the time spent was happy, as she felt relieved to have left the "dry spell" behind her. "I often bring it with me," Judy says, "when I teach and lecture, and I often tell the story of its creation. I call the quilt 'Tears; A Healing Quilt' because the process of making it marked a certain stage in the grieving process, and the fact that I was able to resume design work, indicated to me that I was beginning to heal. When I share the quilt's story, I can always tell which quilters in the audience have already lost their mothers, because they are the ones who shed a tear and come up for a hug after the lecture.

"I sell most of my quilts eventually, but 'Tears' will never be for sale. In fact, no one has ever inquired about purchasing it, probably because it is such a personal work. This is a quilt that really touches people. They don't even have to know the story to respond to it. It has an aura and some special magic. Somehow, all of the emotions that are wrapped up in this quilt are obvious to others.

"For me, it is special because it's the quilt that got me back on track. It marks my emergence as a quilter creating more personal and emotional quilts, so it is important to me not only personally, but professionally."

"Final Flight"

2000, by Judy B. Dales, Kingwood, Texas. Photography by M3 Photographic.

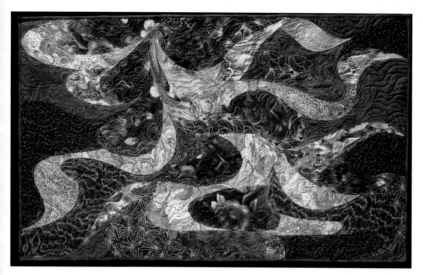

comprehend," Judy B. Dales said. "I couldn't believe she was gone.

"In January of 2000, I went on the annual Caribbean cruise that Doreen and I had attended together for years. Megan, Doreen's daughter, brought some of Doreen's ashes, and we quilters held a small ceremony to honor Doreen's memory.

"As we gathered at the ship's stern, we shared a few words and Megan released the ashes. Expecting them to drop straight down and disappear from sight, I was quite enchanted to see them captured by the breeze, lifted up and away, each little puff drifting off in another direction. This is the moment I have tried to capture in 'Final Flight.' It symbolizes the ongoing journey of the soul, and my hope that Doreen's spirit also flies free and unencumbered."

"Final Flight" was made in memory of Judy B. Dales' beloved friend, Doreen Speckmann, who died suddenly in 1999. "Doreen's death was difficult for me to

"Wear a Pink Ribbon"

1995 by Elizabeth Hendrix, Kent, Washington.

This quilt is about breast cancer. "Over the image of a large floral breast float four generations of women in my family," Elizabeth Hendrix said. "Some have been conquered by breast cancer, and others were challenged and survived. Some, including myself, have undergone multiple surgeries, only to be assured that all is benign. Each story is told in the stitching.

"Floral fabrics seemed uniquely suited to portray this feminine issue which haunts us all."

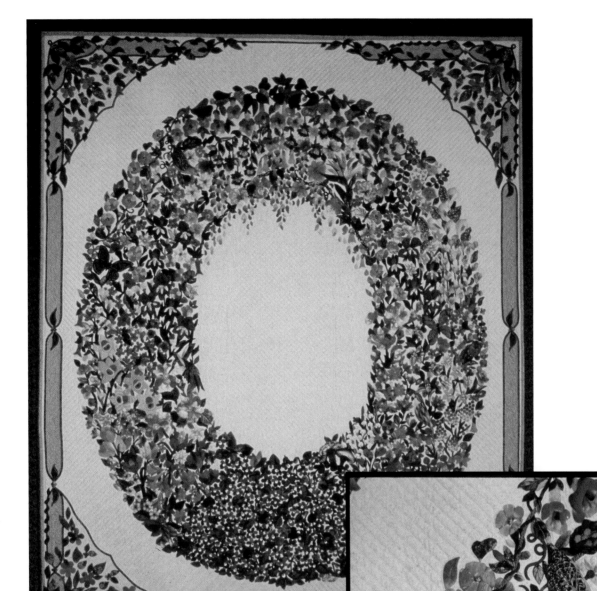

"Violets for Wendy ... Walk Into the Light"

by Lois French, New South Wales.

"Violets for Wendy ... Walk Into the Light" was begun in a journey of grief and growing for Lois French as well as a tribute to her youngest sister's faith, courage, spirit, dignity, and humor cut short by cancer. Lois' daughter, Kate, wrote in *Down Under Quilts*, December 1997-February 1998, "Violets for Wendy was always a source of comfort—a safe place to go when things seemed to get too hard. Lois felt that Wendy was with her as she sewed and wasn't sure that she ever really wanted the quilt to end." On the 1998 American Quilters Society quilt show form, Lois commented that, "the day it was finished, she cried because she knew that it was time to let go and stand on her own."

"Heart of Lightness"

1995 by Natasha Kempers-Cullen, Topsham, Maine.

"Heart of Lightness" is a celebration of Natasha Kempers-Cullen's mother's life. "When I started to make this quilt shortly after Mom's sudden and untimely death," Natasha said, "I thought it would be a requiem, a sad and somber work. I soon realized, however, that Mom's spirit was very much in evidence throughout the making of the piece. Mom was a lively, happy, generous, gregarious, and loving person. A somber quilt just would not come into being! As I was making this piece, I experienced joy and healing. I felt as if Mom and I were in constant, loving conversation. Distraught as I was, and continue to be, by her absence, the month-long period during which "we" made this quilt was an oasis. The aqua cross, which forms part of the background area, is Mom's favorite color and it represents her strong affiliation with the Unitarian Universalist Church. Mom was dedicated to community. She had an uncanny knack of making and keeping friends throughout the world. For me, the cross also represents this ability of hers to achieve community. Mom is the lovely, open figure in the center of the quilt. The world is in her, on her chest. This is the symbol of the Beyond War organization, of which Mom was an active member. The four angels are her four children (we are and were no angels, so I'm guessing she simply saw us that way: A mother's unconditional love!). Mom was very gifted at making braided rugs, and so I created my own interpretation of her braids along either side of the piece. At the bottom of the quilt, the bones symbolize the life-death-life cycle. The urns depict her love of history and art. The goddess figures symbolize her strength as a woman to do whatever she wanted to do. She was not intimidated at all by the fact that she was

'just a woman.' The snakes represent her ability to transform negatives into positives, to always see the good side of any situation. The water beneath her feet symbolizes the oceans, which connect (not separate!) her and all the friends she had all over the world. Toward the end of putting together all of this imagery, I hesitated to add the brightly-colored heart. I wondered if it would be too cute. As I stood considering this possibility, I got shivers all up and down my body. That little heart gave me the obvious title and the spirit of this quilt: Heart of Lightness. This was the title of the book Mom had written not so long ago about her delightful experiences as a Peace Corps volunteer when she was 50 years old! At first, I was worried about plagiarism, but I then realized Mom would be so happy to 'share' the title. Mom is here in this quilt, and I love seeing aspects of her each time I walk by it."

"Stephanie's Quilt"

1995 by Natasha Kempers-Cullen, Topsham, Maine.

"'Stephanie's Quilt' is for my dear friend, made at her request for her funeral," Natasha Kempers-Cullen said. "It is to be draped over her coffin. Stephanie has been diagnosed with terminal cancer. She is 37 years old. She is a beautiful, generous, vivacious person. When she first asked me to create this piece, I was overwhelmed, but I immediately agreed. It became a collaborative project, strengthening and deepening our relationship over the course of the six months it took to make the work. One of the first things I knew must be included in the work was the small composition Stephanie made during a class with me in the summer of 2000. It is at the top center of the quilt. One of the things she realized after making this small panel was that it was the image of a gravestone. How prophetic. She told me that she wanted to have a large tree of life image in this quilt. She wanted the quilt to represent her life, not her death. There are several additional symbolic images: The blue house, the world, the Jewish star, Moose, their dog, the large heart, which symbolizes her grandmother, the lines of people (her family).

"Stephanie sent me a package of beautiful batik fabrics to include in the work. They were perfect for leaves, which are scattered over the whole surface. I added the stones, symbolizing our journey from and return to the earth. There is a tattoo image on the tree trunk, 'I love my Stinko.' Stephanie and her husband call each other by that, very affectionately.

The yellow panel behind the tree is there at her insistence because she likes the energy and colorfulness it displays. I had originally thought I would place pieces of her own fabrics behind the tree, but she insisted on this instead.

"The making of this piece filled me with both joy and despair. I was on a roller coaster of emotions. During the course of creating it, we both decided that it had become a celebration of life, of Stephanie's life. It is not a dirge. Still, upon its completion, we were both nervous, sad, worried. Happily, Stephanie is still very much with us and can enjoy her quilt. Hopefully, its intended use will not present itself for a good, long time."

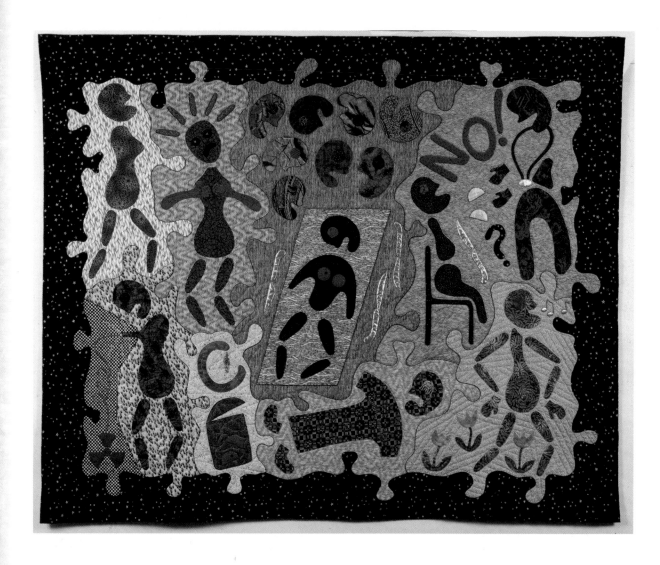

"The Mastectomy"
1995 by Suzanne Marshall, Clayton, Missouri.

"This quilt was made for several reasons," Suzanne Marshall said. "First, I wanted to attempt making a non-traditional quilt and decided to try something in narrative form. Second, since my bilateral mastectomy five years ago, I have been alarmed when hearing stories about women who have found lumps but have not sought treatment because of an overwhelming fear of disfigurement. I hoped to portray a positive message in a quilt—a changed body isn't what is important—*life is*! Third, I hoped to make a quilt that would stimulate conversation about a topic not discussed very much. And fourth, I have a concern that many women do not realize that they have a real choice regarding implants or cosmetic surgery. It is not necessary to conform to society's image.

"The quilt is stitched (all hand appliquéd and hand quilted) in puzzle form—after all, a diagnosis of breast cancer is something of a puzzle, and needs to be taken one step at a time.

"The narrative for the quilt reads from left to right. The first piece depicts a healthy, whole woman, walking along with everything okay in her world. Then she gets a mammogram. She receives a diagnosis. She has the surgery. There is a puzzle piece with her in her hospital gown showing the stitches where she had the mastectomy. In the upper right-hand corner she has gone back to the doctor who asks her if she would like to have more surgery for implants. She says, '*No!*' The lower right-hand puzzle piece is the message of the quilt. It portrays the figure with a changed body but definitely enjoying life amidst flowers and music."

"Sliding Goddess with Heart"
Ruth B. McDowell

"I made this quilt for my good friend Doreen Speckmann," Ruth H. McDowell said, "developed from a drawing of a photograph taken, by Margaret Peters, of Doreen teaching a group of quilters to dance 'The Electric Slide' at the Empty Spools Symposium at Asilomar in California.

"Doreen lighted up any group she was part of, and was a great and joyful dancer. I sent her the quilt as a surprise gift to a good friend. It was one of her favorite things. Of course, I had no idea that Doreen would die so young. Sometimes you get lucky, and do the right thing at the right time. This was one of those times."

"On Wednesday Morning"
Yvonne Porcella, Modesto, California
Photograph by Sharon Risedorph

In response to the 1995 bombing of the Alfred P. Murrah building in Oklahoma City, Oklahoma, Yvonne Porcella of Modesta, California, made "On Wednesday Morning" to honor the children who died in the bombing. Now in the collection of the Museum of the American Quilter's Society, Paducah, Kentucky, sponsored in part by Dr. Gerald and Arlene Blackburn. The Museum of American Quilter's Society, in celebrating its tenth anniversary, has acquired this quilt for its permanent collection.

PHOTO GALLERY

"Nocturnal Garden"

Ted Storm-van Weelden, Netherlands.
Photography by Gerard van Yperen

Ted Storm-van Weelden, of the Netherlands, says: "Quilting creates a rhythm of reflection; it is my way to unwind." Never having used black fabrics before, she created "Nocturnal Garden"; it was awarded 2001 Best of Show by That Patchwork Place at the International Quilt Festival in Houston, Texas. Ted feels that making the quilt was a personal challenge to persevere through the aches and pains of aging and the menopausal effects of stress and depression. In her words, she "always found this quilt as a safe friend waiting for me, accepting gracefully my anger, my tears, my unsure mind. It's reflected in the quilt: The black for darkness, the Shi Sha mirrors as my tears. Working over four years I healed, my quilt grew to be beautiful and I matured. 'Nocturnal Garden' is a quilt to enjoy, to comfort, a quilt to heal, in which the tiny mirrors now represent sparkles of life."

"The Beat Goes On"

by Ricky Tims

"The Beat Goes On" by Ricky Tims. Says Ricky of its creation: "In April 2000, I underwent unexpected quadruple heart bypass surgery. On day eight following the surgery, I began this quilt to commemorate the event. The top was finished four days later, thanks in part to my visiting parents. My Dad tore fabric strips (my arms could not manage that motion) and my Mom kept me fed with healthy meals. The title is after the popular Sonny and Cher song."

"Far and Away"
by Judith Vierow

"'Far and Away' was created in response to a call for quilts following the bombing of the Federal Building in Oklahoma City, and traveled in the show of quilts about that terrible event," Judith Vierow said. "I was working in Vermont at the time and had only the rudiments of a studio at hand. But I knew I had the fabric and dyes as well as many leaves for printing. I chose leaves for their obvious transcendence of the physical world; they exist so short a time and then are gone. They seemed a perfect symbol for the lives lost in Oklahoma City, particularly the lives of the children. The text came from my own impressions of the event. It was worked on over a few days, brought home, and finished. In all its aspects it relies on simplicity. Nothing fancy. A wholecloth quilt.

"I hope it meant something to those who experienced the event and its aftermath first hand. To those of us who merely watched in horror on television or read about it in the news, it could never have the same impact as it would for those who lived it. But there is a sympathy here; an empathy, perhaps a suggestion of healing."

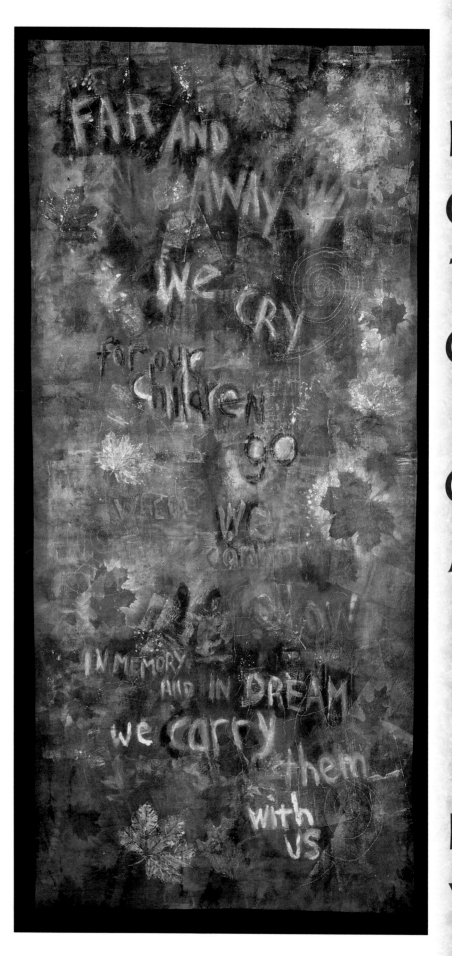

A Brief History
of Burial Quilts, Memorial Quilts,
and Celebratory Quilts

Circa 1880, coffin cover with ornately embroidered velvets, silks, and satin. Motifs are scrolls, florals, and grapes over the head area. Note the black silk covered scallops and elaborate stitching. Photograph used with permission of the International Quilt Study Center at the University of Nebraska-Lincoln.

In the Beginning

The phrase "ashes to ashes, dust to dust" is often repeated at the time of one's final journey, the funeral. Similarly, one could say we are born into the warmth and protection of a quilt. Many of our ancestors left this life in the same warmth, comfort, and protection of either a casket quilt to be buried with, or a commemorative memorial quilt made in their honor as a way to ease the quiltmaker's grief. Humans may begin as microscopic

beings growing and being nurtured in a warm environment but, nine months later, babies are thrust into a world that is at least twenty-five degrees colder than their mother's womb before being gently wrapped in a much welcomed hospital-microwaved blanket to soothe their miraculous entry. Often our babies are taken home in a quilt, while others born at home are immediately enveloped in a quilt's protective warmth.

From the time before Christ or slightly after, 100 B.C.E.-200 A.C.E., a crosshatched and contour quilted textile was found in the tomb of a Scythian chieftain. The Academy of Sciences in Russia calls it a "funerary carpet" and has proved that using burial textiles is an ancient custom.[1] Even Jesus' body was covered with a linen shroud commonly called the Shroud of Turin.[2]

Time Honored International Customs and Traditions

Throughout the last two millennia, international examples of burial textiles have been well documented by archeologists, ethnologists, and sociologists – among other disciplinary experts. All were intended to ready the makers for their own final journeys both spiritually and decoratively, be made for family members, or be commemorative pieces to be used in specific rites and rituals.

C. Oelofsen, funeral director and embalmer of Kitwe in northern Rhodesia, reported adult South African Afrikaners can purchase coffins either lined in white calico or embossed silk. For children twenty years old or younger, a white coffin is covered with embossed swansdown, a soft, thick cloth mixed with silk, rayon, or cotton.[3]

In Denmark, coffins are fitted with bed linens, and it is common practice in rural areas for young women to make their burial dresses to be used years later.[4] In contrast, Sula Benet, author of *Song, Dance and Custom of Peasant Poland* writes that burial outfits "as fine as can be afforded" were discussed and constructed by most older women.[5]

At least in rural Hungary, some widows after age forty make a hand embroidered white death cloth, a centuries-old tradition. It is used for an adult, while a dying child is covered with its mother's fancy wedding shawl and bridal head wreath. Another special cover is used as a bridge to the afterlife when it adorns a fresh grave.[6] Similarly, as in Hungary, deceased peasant Rumanians

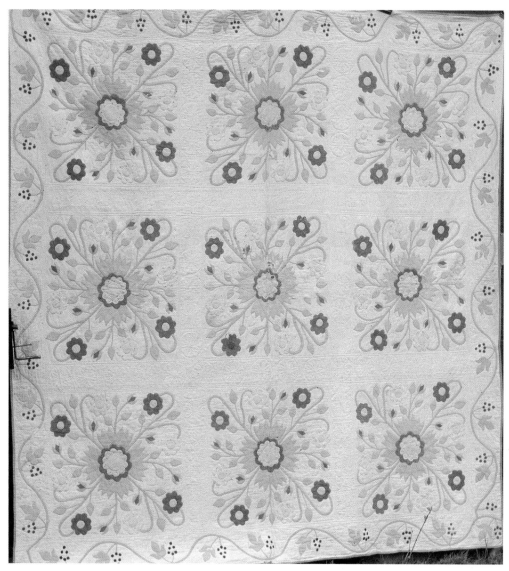

1851 "Oregon Rose." Made by friends, neighbors, and relatives for Jacob and Sarah Robbins and their nine children before they migrated from Indiana to Oregon over the Oregon Trail in 1852. Permission granted by the Mollala Area Historical Society Dibble House, Mollala, Oregon.

wear a specially made death shirt, and the coffin is lined with a "giulgin," a shroud or winding sheet. Yugoslavians have also created fine body covers among other needs for their final journeys.[7]

American anthropologist Charles Wagley writes of a rural Guatemalan practice of laying out the body on a "blanket-covered bench." Also, older women in Santiago Chimaltenango weave their elaborate funeral blouses, "huipils," in advance of need.[8]

Since the eighteenth century in America, quilt-makers have made quilts for domestic, utilitarian, friendship, and decorative needs. Some were made specifically to honor rites of passage such as weddings, a young man's freedom or migration to the West.

Casket covers, mourning memorial quilts, and banners recording the lives of family members were also made and are now rare finds. Women have sought through the labor of their hands to work through the grief of their hearts. Sometimes utilitarian quilts wrapped loved ones, and were buried with the deceased. For example, three daughters of Nathaniel Robbins (Jacob's cousin) succumbed to cholera on the Oregon

Wagon wheels in quilting.

Granddaughter of quilt maker Margaret Stewart Hughes, Helen (Aldrich) Noteboom stands in front of the quilt partially made of the white silk casket lining used in 1904 for her great-grandmother, Margaret MacIntire Stewart's casket. Quilt owned by Christine Dietsch, Tuscaloosa, Alabama.

Silk and watercolor on silk Mourning Picture, c. 1804-1810, 20-1/4" by 21-3/16", by Maria Pomroy. Permission granted by the St. Louis Art Museum. Gift of Mrs. Stratford Lee Morton in memory of Stratford Lee Morton..

Trail and were buried together in a wagon box fitted with a mattress and covered with quilts and blankets as cited by Mary Bywater Cross in *Treasures in the Trunk: Quilts of the Oregon Trail.*[9]

Other quiltmakers were able to express their grief in mourning and memorial quilts such as in a quilt made by Tamar Horton Harris of North's Landing, Indiana for her daughter Grace Gertrude North. It includes memorial symbols of embroidered calla lilies, a painted angel, and pieces of her dresses with lace also made by her mother. Amelia Peck writes in *American Quilts & Coverlets In the Metropolitan Museum of Art*, "Through diaries, it is known that at times of sorrow, sewing seemed to be a great comfort to the nineteenth-century woman."[10]

Unlike some Native American Indian, Polynesian, and Asian cultures described in Carol Williams Gebel's article, "Final Rites of Passage Quilts" in *Uncoverings 1995*,[11] casket and mourning memorial quilts are somewhat rare in America's Anglo-Saxon culture. This is most probably because needlework memorial samplers from the eighteenth and nineteenth centuries were a more common way to record family histories and to express grief. That is not to say that making these quilts was rarely done since there are surviving examples still being passed on within families.

Crazy quilt coffin cover owned by Carole Samples, Omaha, Nebraska. It is backed with casket lining and was made in the late 19th century by the Libertine sisters of Missouri. They never married and always lived together. Each made their own fan, and the cover was to be used at each of their funerals.

In the early decades of the 1800s, death was viewed as a release of earthly bonds; the real life we all should look forward to was in Heaven with God.

The monument, pictured at right, is reminiscent of nineteenth century mourning sentiments. Such a great deal of sentimentality was associated with the deceased and the dying process itself that during Eli Lilly's last illness in Baltimore in 1847, nine of his eleven children, their spouses and friends came together to make a floral appliqué quilt complete with a swag border. It was signed by all, even Lilly himself, on the lyre block during his final months.[12] When indelible ink became available in the mid-1830s, memorial verses and mourning symbols such as willow trees, engraved urns and monuments, and grieving family members began to appear in quilt blocks. According to herbalist and author Ellen Evert Hopman, *Tree Medicine Tree Magic*, the Celts and Druids of ancient Europe held nine trees sacred. Among them, the willow and yew trees had special properties. Hopman cites folklore stating people carried a piece of willow with them in order to ease the fear of death. Bark from the tree was often used in funeral pyres. Also, in Europe, the yew was known as the tree of immortality and was planted in graveyards along with the willow.[13]

She Mourned Him for Forty Years

Queen Victoria of Great Britain ascended to the throne in 1839, and married her first cousin Albert in 1840. He died in 1861 and Victoria mourned him for forty years. At Windsor Castle, where Albert had died, the servants were instructed to wear arm bands of black crepe for eight years. In 1863, for the wedding of the Prince of Wales, the bride and bridegroom were relieved of mourning, but the royal princesses all wore shades of half-mourning at the insistence of the Queen, who sat isolated from the rest of the congregation, still in deep mourning. She would wear mourning for Albert until her own death in 1901."[14] The Queen always wore a black silk dress and white cap, kept rooms full of mementos, photographs, busts, and miniatures. She even laid out Albert's clothes on his bed at Windsor Castle every night, and in the morning, fresh water was put in his basin. She slept with his photograph, over her head, taken of his head and shoulders as he lay dead.

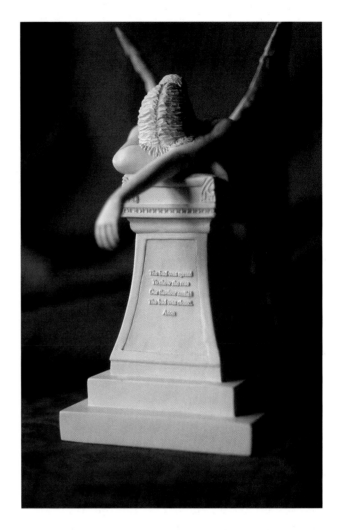

Inspired by Victorian turn-of-the-century monuments in the northeastern England village of Ryhope, artist Alan Dickinson's twenty-first century cast resin statue of a bereaved angel mourning on a monument is engraved, 'The bud was spread to show the rose, Our Savior smiled, the bud was closed.' Anonymous.

Daguerreotype of an unknown loved one in a velvet lined heavenly harp mourning frame. Author's collection.

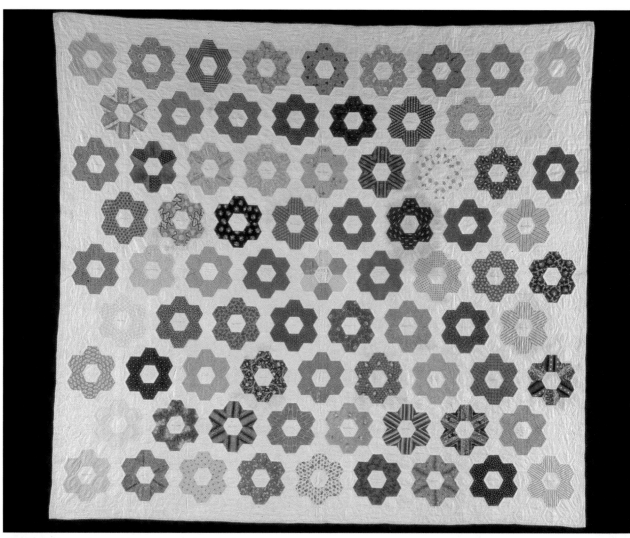

Jennette Crossman Evans "Memorial Dear Little Charlie Quilt," 1865-1870. Los Angeles County Museum of Art, Gift of Richard and Cynthia Jones. Photograph ©2002 Museum Associates/LACMA.

Quilts in "Memento Mori"

David E. Stanner, author of "Sex, Death and Daguerreotypes: Toward an Understanding of Image as Elegy" in *America and the Daguerreotype*, gives insight into the reasons behind photographing the deceased. Stanner maintains such photography was a way of keeping the loved one alive for the remaining grieving family. Several museums and private collectors have daguerreotypes showing both children and adults with quilts either draped over or under them or used as backdrops. The Strong Museum of Rochester, New York has an extensive collection.

Jennette Evans sadly inscribed three blocks in her quilt recording the death dates of her two little boys, Charlie and Franky:

'Dear little Charlie / died Oct 28th 1852
/ Aged two years and / six months. /-
/ The grave is not my / loved ones
home'

'Dear Little Franky, died Jan 19th 1855.
/ Aged three years, He is an angel
/ now.'
Then thirteen years later, she wrote of her husband:
"In memory / of / Robert L. Evans.
/My dear husband / who died Jan 23rd / 1865.

There is rest for the weary." [15]

On another block she wrote:
"My Robert. / I will meet thee in / Heaven"[16]

These "memento mori" daguerreotypes fell out of fashion at about the time of the Civil War, when retouching and mass production techniques became available. But photographs of the dead retained a certain popularity, in rural communities and among some urban poor, well into the twentieth century. Perhaps this was a carry-over among European immigrants—particularly those from Mediterranean countries, where postmortem photography began to be popular *after* the First World War.[17] Today,

especially since the resurgence of quilting in the 1970s and the formation of quilting guilds across the nation, some families of various religious backgrounds and cultures continue to photograph their loved ones in the casket, with or without quilts.

Although created and photographed after the actual death, Bets Ramsey of Nashville, Tennessee, was commissioned by Episcopalian minister Charles Carter to appliqué a white wool crepe funeral pall in memory of his father and in celebration of his life.

Reverend Carter donated the pall to the Brush Hill Cumberland Presbyterian Church in Nashville, and it is now used in congregation members' funerals. According to Ramsey, "The border motifs illustrate excerpts from the gospel according to St. Matthew; 'Pearls before Swine,' etc." In 1992, Ramsey was commissioned by Esther Duncan to create "The Angels." Later, it was shown in a major exhibition at the Tennessee State Museum in Nashville. In 1999, it was the pulpit hanging for Esther's fineral, where some of her own quilts were also displayed.

Album Epitaphs

Extending the Victorian album book rage to some friendship album quilts, messages in indelible ink from the maker's friends even contained references to the life eternal: "An interest in your Prayers I crave /That we may meet beyond the grave."[18] This inscription was written by Elizabeth Ann Culver of Patapsco Station in 1845 on the "Eggleston Bed Cover" owned by Mr. & Mrs. Thomas H. Morgan. It was quite common to collect scraps of cloth from near and distant, alive and deceased relatives' clothing to be used and labeled as such in album and signature quilts. Barbara Brackman, in *An Encyclopedia of Pieced Quilt Patterns,* recorded a block called "Memory Wreath," which was first identified by Ruth Finley as being made of the deceased's clothing.

"The Angels," 1992 by Bets Ramsey, Chattanooga, Tennessee.

Memory Wreath block.

Brackman also recorded Carrie Hall identifying an Album Memory Wreath block which frequently contained scraps of clothing from the loved one.

During the last two years of her life, thirty year old Eliza Naudain Corbit of Delaware became an invalid. Wanting family and familiarity around her, she pieced eighty-one blocks for a signature album quilt and sent them to family and friends for signing. She lived long enough to sash and set them together and ink her epitaph in 1844. A portion of the quilt reads:

"Thus far the Lord hath led me on, Thus far his power prolongs my days, and every evening shall make known /Some fresh memorial of his grace. Much of my time has run to waste, and I perhaps are near my home:

But he forgives my follies past, and gives me strength for days to come. I lay my body down to sleep, Peace is the pillow for my head: While well-appointed angels keep/ Their watchful stations round my bed. Thus when the night of death shall come /My flesh shall rest beneath the ground /And wait the voice to rouse my tomb, with sweet salvation in the sound."

She did not live to see her final journey quilt set in the frame as the "night of death" came for Eliza in 1844.[19]

Eliza Naudain Corbit's Signature quilt. Courtesy of Winterthur Museum.

Daguerreotype of an unknown woman, probably on her death bed. Courtesy of Julian Wolfe, Wantagh, New York. Taking photographs of loved ones on their death beds wasn't an unusual practice.

Even presentation quilts to ministers sometimes contained memorial verses for founding families such as in the 1846-1850 Sewing Society quilt of the First Baptist Church of Philadelphia. The wreaths contain names of honored and memorialized founding church members. Although this quilt most probably was not made specifically to aid the mourning or grieving process, it nonetheless shows that the deceased founding members were revered, memorialized, and commemorated in a quilt for their efforts and contributions to the church.

The Sewing Society Quilt marked, "1846-1850 Philadelphia, Pennsylvania First Baptist Church." Photo by permission of the Philadelphia Museum of Art.

Another exquisite example of honoring the dead in textile form is the "Quaker Silk Quilt," made about 1850 in Pennsylvania and New Jersey. M.91.230 Quaker Memorial/Friendship Quilt (detail, above), 19th century, England, London. Los Angeles County Museum Associates/LACMA.

Detail image;inscription reads: "To my sister Hannah Ann Ellis/Tho' nipp'd be the delicate bud/That to our affection was given/Yet tis joyful to feel that tis cherished above/And yielding sweet inosense in heaven."[20]

M.87.175 Friendship Quilt, "Quaker Mourning"(detail), circa 1847 United States. Los Angeles County Museum of Art, gift of Mr. and Mrs. Laurence A. Ferris. Photograph @2002 Museum Associates/ LACMA.)21

From 1841-1847; by Mary P. Allen. Mary created her "Friendship album Quaker Mourning Quilt," with the following inscription:

10th Mo 1847-
Mary P Allen
I will not mourn my griefs below
Nor all their baneful train
But hope at last to meet above
My early Friends again.

At least two quilts classified as Baltimore Albums honoring two revered Baltimore soldiers who died in the Mexican War are called "The Lieutenant-Colonel Watson Memorial Quilt" and "The Major Samuel Ringgold Memorial Quilt" because they contain inscribed monument blocks fashioned after a temporary monument in the Baltimore Merchants Exchange building where Major Ringgold lay in state in December 1846. Collectively, hundreds of grieving, mourning hours were spent on these quilts honoring the deceased and easing the grief of the makers. The Snyder Memorial bed cover, made shortly after 1845, includes family vital statistics in the center medallion block. The album blocks surrounding it contain other names, verses, and inked drawings.

"The Major Samuel Ringgold Memorial Quilt." Marked "S.A.W.L." Assembly and quilting attributed to Sarah Anne Whittington Lankford of Baltimore, Maryland, circa 1850. Permission granted by Abby Aldrich Rockefeller Folk Art Museum, Williamsburg, Virginia.[22]

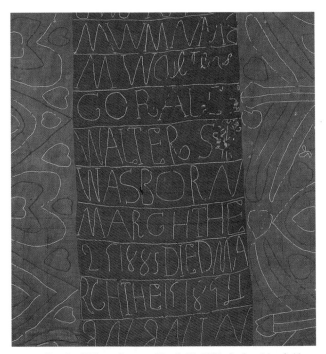

CoraLee Walters (born on March 29, 1885, died on March 19, 1894, at nearly nine years of age), was mourned in an 80 inch by 72 inch primitive embroidered strip quilt. Because of its size, it may have been used as her funeral pall or casket cover. It is now owned by the Rocky Mountain Quilt Museum in Golden, Colorado, but former owner, Betsy Caprio Hedberg, said its documentation suggests it was a Kentucky quilt. Permission granted by Rocky Mountain Quilt Museum, Golden, Colorado.

Commemorative Quilts Honor People and Events

Both the Lieutenant-Colonel Watson and Major Samuel Ringgold Memorial quilts can also be classified as commemorative pieces since they honor and remember an historical event. In comparison, in 1998, Serena Strother Wilson of Columbus, Ohio, decided to share her freed slave-born great-grandmother Eliza Farrow's Secret Quilt Code. In the early- to mid-nineteenth century, Eliza learned the patterns while still in Africa. With the aid of other slaves, she developed them into quilt blocks to help other enslaved African-Americans escape South Carolina and Georgia. The block names and spiritual songs they were allowed to sing conveyed secret messages to prospective escapees. Wilson said, "The fabrics they used often were scraps saved from torn shirts or dresses of a loved one who had been sold. These quilters stitched their love, prayers, and memories into pieced sampler quilts and, according to the oral history that has been passed down in my family, these quilts were used to communicate information on when and how to escape on the Underground Railroad." Eliza was married to a free black man who bought her freedom after seven years, but they stayed in South Carolina where he was a blacksmith and preacher. The Secret Quilt Code that Eliza made and carried with her when visiting other plantations to surreptitiously teach the code commemorated her braveness, fortitude, and tenacity in helping others escape to freedom

on the Underground Railroad, and memorialized those who had lived and died as slaves. Serena learned the code as it had been passed on orally to her grandmother, Nora Bell Farrow McDaniel:

The Monkey Wrench turns the Wagon Wheel north, up the road toward Canada. Follow the Drunkard's Path, watch, and pray. Look for the Flying Geese in the day and the North Star at night. Follow the Bear's Paw trail to the Crossroads. Shoofly says dress up; put on cotton or satin Bow Ties, Sue Bonnets, or Bandannas. Soon, you will cross over Jordan. Look for the Tumbling Blocks. Nearby you will see a cathedral with the Dresden Plate window. Now go in, you can sing and shout, 'Thank God, I Be Free!' You can get married, exchange Rings, no more Irish Chains around your feet. You can build a Log Cabin; the women can dig and plant a Nine Patch garden. When you get hot, you can Fan. The men can go fishing in a Sailboat, and the children can play with Pinwheels. When somebody dies, weave a sweet grass Basket, put wildflowers in it, and put it on the grave. You and your children can never be sold away again. It will always be howdy and never good-bye! Thank God You Be Free![23]

Native American Giveaway Ceremonies

While some European-descended Americans have used quilts in funerary practices for the past 200 years, several other cultures, including some North American Indian tribes, have used them commonly either as shrouds, cushions, coffin palls, or wall hangings during the funeral rite itself or during the first anniversary memorial celebration of the death.[24] Before Europeans came in contact with the Plains Indians of North America and tried to introduce, and then force, their religious beliefs upon them, tribes such as the Delaware, Shawnee, Lakota, and Ogalala Sioux practiced Giveaway ceremonies for such life events as naming or honoring and also at the time of death or later. At funerals, quilts covered the casket as well as hung behind it. Depending on the traditions of the tribe, items of the deceased could be given away at the funeral ceremony or be destroyed. A Giveaway memorial service, sometimes as long as a year after the death, could occur as an anniversary observance. Among today's Lakota and Ogalala Sioux, quilts – especially star quilts – still are the most prestigious of Giveaway gifts.[25]

Because of trading with the Euro-Americans, the Eastern Dakota Santee Sioux of Griswold, Manitoba, began to wrap bodies in blankets instead of buffalo hides or deer skins, which allowed the folds to be stuffed with personal possessions; in the case of a deceased woman, her sewing tools were included. By 1952, quilts were commonly used to shroud bodies, and new quilts were used to cover the grave at the ceremony ending the mourning period. The Santees continue to practice Giveaway memorial services during which, among other items, quilts are prized gifts. The Santees of Prairie Island and Morton, Minnesota, have Giveaway ceremonies on the first anniversary after death.[26]

Quilts in Burial Rites and Funeral Memorabilia

One ancient burial practice common to other cultures seems to have been used after George and Abigail Malick arrived in the Oregon territory in 1848 from Illinois (originally from Pennsylvania), with six of their seven children. When George died in 1854, daughter Rachel wrote her married sister back in Illinois that their mother would send "some of our morning dresses and some of his shroud."[27] Could Rachel have meant "m-o-u-r-n-i-n-g" dresses? Cloth from family members, both living and dead, was often put in album quilts and labeled with their names. In this way, a quiltmaker could give a temporary immortality to a loved one in the form of a quilt or casket cover to be passed on and used by other family members. Indeed, some quilts have been made with the funeral ribbons used to decorate floral wreaths and casket sprays or other funeral arrangements such as casket pillows, hair barrettes, and funerary jewelry. Excess casket lining material was used by Polly Taylor and her daughter, Nancy Taylor Ruff, along with a piece of the shroud Polly's husband was wrapped in to make a crazy quilt called "The Shroud Quilt."[28]

1895 California Crazy Memorial quilt depicting a mourning ribbon of Ulysses S. Grant.

Satin, silk, and wool casket quilt made by Sarah B. Chapman, 1802-1902 of Bethel, Vermont. Pinned mini-quilt label contains her vital statistics. It was passed down within the family and used again and again. Collection of author.

Late nineteenth century crazy quilt in the collection of Marilyn Woodin of Kalona, Iowa. Note black coffins in lower row.

Mrs. Ervin (Dorothy) Jordan standing by a black and white Lone Star quilt made by her husband's great-great-grandmother Sarah Leggett, for her son, Irvin. This circa 1860 Lone Star quilt was never used because Irvin died after modern lined coffins were readily available and affordable.

Marilyn Woodin of Woodin Wheel Antiques in Kalona, Iowa, sold a crazy quilt incorporating human hair in one embroidery motif.

Another of Marilyn Woodin's crazy mourning quilts depicts a center block of shredded ribbon, possibly showing a face or inked message, surrounded by the grief-resolving colors of lavender, pink, and white, and in the bottom row black embroidered caskets. Also seen are a snake indicating death, typical white funeral flowers, and the deceased's initials. The embroidered fan depicting the River Styx with the ship to heaven and ship to hell are shown.

Many Americans traveling the Overland Trail in the mid-1800s wanted their loved ones buried in a warm quilt since they hadn't the time or resources to bury them in a coffin. Indeed, the practice of being ever-ready for any untimely tragedy compelled "Sarah Leggett of Kountze, Texas, to make nine identical black and white Lone Star quilts for use in the future to wrap the bodies of her children before placement in their pine box caskets whenever needed. At least one not used for that purpose has survived from the nineteenth century."[29]

Mourning, Memorial and Casket Quilts

Patsy and Myron Orlofsky write in *Quilts in America* that a mourning or widow quilt was used by the bereaved during the mourning period. It is not known if they were made before the death or after, but those identified were said to be made during the Civil War with black and white fabrics, sometimes gray, but usually with a black border. The patterns used were a dart motif to signify the black darts of death or a Cross-and-Star. Weeping willows, harps, and lyres were common quilting designs.[30]

The most famous funeral/mourning-memorial quilt in existence today is probably Elizabeth Roseberry Mitchell's "Graveyard Quilt" completed in 1843. Beginning with the deaths of two boys among her thirteen children, Elizabeth would bring basted coffins from the border area into the family plot in the center of the quilt and label their vital statistics on paper pinned to the appliquéd coffins. It is a medallion quilt with its center motif a gated fence illustrating an enclosed family plot in a graveyard. It includes four named coffins and delicate floral embroidery intertwined in the fence, with each corner showing a large tombstone. Variable Stars offset with plain printed fabric blocks fill out the rest of the quilt body. The borders include basted appliqué named coffins waiting to be added to the center graveyard as each relative makes his final journey. The edge of the borders show a final fenced area, presumably the cemetery, with an appliqué fenced and floral embroidered pathway that interrupts the bottom three rows of Variable Star and plain blocks, and then enters the family plot area at the quilt's center. In Linda Otto Lipsett's 1995 book *Elizabeth Roseberry Mitchell's Graveyard Quilt: An American Pioneer Saga*, reference is made to "old timers in the Appalachian area, who have vague and various memories of such a quilt to remember the dead and to record and mark the place where a loved one was buried."[31] According to some, the graveyard section of the quilt was made quickly and put over the body at the funeral, then hung over the back of the settee or chair in mourning. Lipsett observed, "Truly, her quilt was not a quilt of death but a quilt preserving the memory of loved ones."[32]

Left: Author's Princess Feather mourning/memorial quilt with several lyres in the quilting.

Above: Detail showing the center lyre having a baby's hand within it seems to indicate the infant's death.

Mid-19th century four-block 'Tree of Life' quilt. Author's collection. Quilting showing babies Keith and Kenneth's hands. There are many hearts in the quilting, which could have celebrated their births or mourned their passing.

Science Enters the Quilting World

For decades, many quiltmakers have said the reason they quilt is that it relaxes them; the act of quilting is a stress reliever. Statements such as "I'd rather quilt than any other technique involved in quilt making because the movements are so relaxing" have been physiologically substantiated in a 1995 clinical study commissioned by the American Home Sewing and Craft Association and conducted by Robert H. Reiner, Ph.D., a faculty member of the Department of Psychiatry at New York University Medical Center. One group, made up of 15 experienced sewers, and the other group of 15 non-sewers, were tested and measured for blood pressure, heart rate, perspiration, and peripheral skin temperature. Sewing, of the five activities that all the women were monitored for before and after engaging in the activity, was measured as the most relaxing: The experienced sewers' heart rates dropped by about eleven beats per minute, and the non-sewers' rates dropped about seven beats per minute. The average heart rate in the other four activities *increased* for all the women four to eight beats per minute.[33]

Elizabeth Roseberry Mitchell's "Graveyard Quilt," 1843, Kentucky. Permission granted by Kentucky Historical Society Special Collections & Archives, Frankfort, Kentucky. This is the most famous funeral/ mourning/memorial quilt in existence today. Beginning with the deaths of two boys among her thirteen children, Elizabeth would bring basted coffins from the border area into the family plot in the center of the quilt and label their vital statistics on paper pinned to the appliqued coffins.

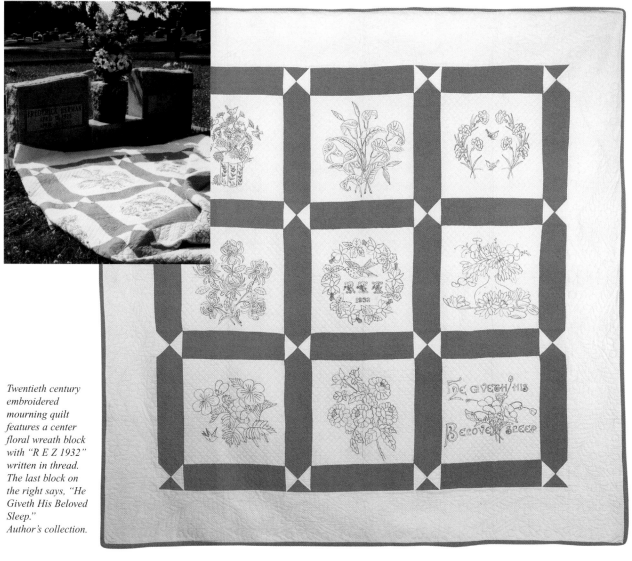

Twentieth century embroidered mourning quilt features a center floral wreath block with "R E Z 1932" written in thread. The last block on the right says, "He Giveth His Beloved Sleep." Author's collection.

Occupational therapists have long assigned "manual arts," such as sewing, to patients of all ages to help facilitate fine motor physical skills or to overcome emotional and or social difficulties.

Modern Quilters Express Grief, Anger, and Sorrow in Special Quilts

American quilters have taken up their needles to express their feelings of grief and/or anger at events occurring all over the world. More recently, expressions of community grief and memorial quilts have followed national outcries about tragedies such as the explosion of the space shuttle Challenger in 1986. In 1987, Cleve Jones of San Francisco, California, initiated the NAMES Project Quilt in memory of AIDS victims to both celebrate their short lives and grieve as the family or friends left behind. To this day, thousands of quilters have participated in this effort. Many guilds across the country have made "ABC" baby quilts for infants born HIV-positive and children living with AIDS.

Quilts made to help the "Quilt For A Cure" breast cancer campaign are sewn to honor guild and family members' battles with the disease, and are raffled to aid research. Portions of the sale of specially designed fabric by designer Bonnie Benn Stratton for Northcott Fabrics are donated to breast cancer research. Stratton continues to create fabric lines for "Quilt For A Cure" after losing a loved one to the disease.

In 1990, wall hangings and quilts were stitched to express the horror of the scenes we saw on television as the Gulf War came into our homes via satellite.

In 1993, when Polly Klaas was abducted and murdered in Petaluma, California, a child asked her quiltmaker mother, Marjorie Bevis, "What can I do for Polly?" She answered, "There's nothing you can do for Polly but there is something we can do for you." Marjorie began making a quilt and 200 blocks were contributed by other children in the school.

In July 1994, central Oregon experienced a terrible forest fire on Storm King Mountain. Nine firefighters from the Hotshots Fire unit lost their lives. Nine quilts were made for the lost firefighters' families.

In 1995, the Oklahoma City bombing of the Alfred P. Murrah Federal Building again prompted quilters to express their grief and subsequent hope and prayers for the survivors and their families. Yvonne Porcella made "On Wednesday Morning" to honor the children who died in the bombing. Judith Vierow was asked to create a quilt for The Oklahoma City Children's Memorial Art Quilts exhibition, titled "Far and Away." (See page 15, Photo Gallery.)

When Princess Diana was tragically killed in 1998, a fabric company came out with a beautiful royal blue background fabric adorned with white roses dedicated to her memory, and grieving fans made many quilted items. Quiltmaker and teacher Barb Vlack, Illinois, states, "I am glad I had this project to occupy me while I attended her funeral on TV."

More recently, the American Quilter's Society Museum asked for quilt blocks expressing quilters' feelings about the teenage shootings at the Paducah, Kentucky, high school that would be made into quilts.

"Violets for Wendy ... Walk Into the Light' was begun in a journey of grief and growing for Lois French, as well as a tribute to her youngest sister's faith, courage, spirit, dignity, and humor cut short by cancer. French's daughter, Kate, wrote in *Down Under Quilts*, December 1997-February 1998 issue, "Violets for Wendy was always a source of comfort – a safe place to go when things seemed to get too hard. Lois felt that Wendy was with her as she sewed and wasn't sure that she ever really wanted the quilt to end." (See page 9, Photo Gallery.)

Ted Storm-van Weelden, Netherlands, says: "Quilting creates a rhythm of reflection, it is my way to unwind." Never having used black fabrics before, she created "Nocturnal Garden," which won the 2001 Best of Show award given by That Patchwork Place at the International Quilt Festival in Houston, Texas. It was a personal challenge to persevere the aches and pains of aging and menopausal effects of stress and depression. (See page 14, Photo Gallery.)

In her words, Ted "always found this quilt as a safe friend waiting for me, accepting gracefully my anger, my tears, my unsure mind. It's reflected in the quilt: the black for darkness, the Shi Sha mirrors as my tears. Working over four years I healed, my quilt grew to be beautiful and I matured ... 'Nocturnal Garden' is a quilt to enjoy, to comfort, a quilt to heal, in which the tiny mirrors now represent sparkles of life."

The 9-11 Quilt Gallery

Within three days of the September 11, 2001 terrorist attacks on New York City's World Trade Center, the Pentagon in Washington, D.C., and the heroic efforts of the passengers on the plane crashing near Pittsburgh, Pennsylvania, Chris Davis and Amy Leasure sent a world-wide e-mail plea for all quilters to help create the World Trade Center Memorial Quilt to be fashioned in the same manner as the multi-paneled AIDS Quilt.

I felt compelled to volunteer to sew twenty-five star blocks into a panel for them. My own sense of needing to contribute to the ease of victims' family and friends' anguished hearts led me to begin the Quilters in Need or "QIN" (pronounced "kin") project. My research for this book after my own grief journey in 1993, the lecturing and the classes I teach, informed me that quilters instinctively turn to their needles in times of sorrow, grief, and anger to express their emotions of resolve, commemoration, and honor. My goal was to supply quilt-making materials to victims' families, and friends who quilted, to encourage them to create quilts as outlets for their myriad feelings about this tragedy. I was a facilitator among my home guild, the Prairie Pine Quilt Guild, the Staten Island Quilt Guild, and Moonlight Quilters of Staten Island (the latter two represented by Jane Johnson, who received and distributed the materials). Our members donated fabrics in fat quarters. Hobbs Fibers in Waco, Texas, donated the batting. The Staten Island quilters decided to make quilts using the materials for non-quilting families of victims.

Author's panel of twenty-five WTCMQ blocks. Theresa Drummond, regional coordinator of the Stafford Piecemakers Quilt Guild, Stafford, Virginia, assembled at least six panels.

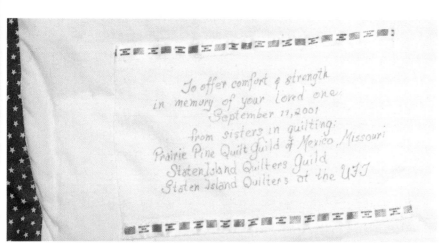

Label on back of Barbara Cohen's Tessellation quilt. Note the "United We Stand" flag ribbons included in each kit.

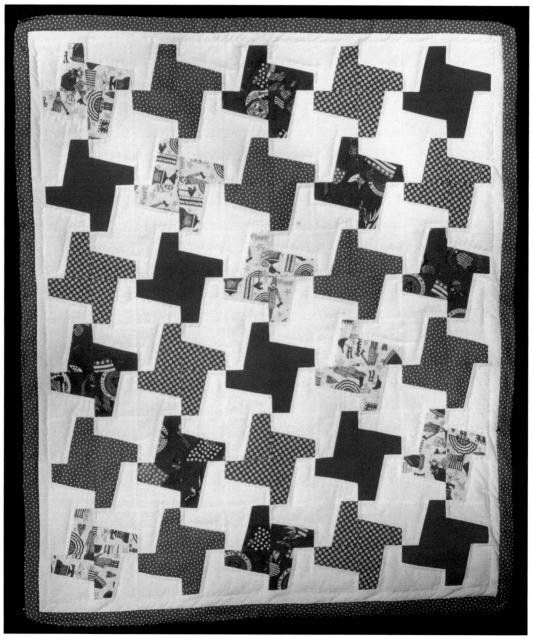

Barbara Cohen's Tessellation quilt , above, was given to a gentleman quilt store owner who had given batting for "Gratitude Quilts" for the families of the eighty rescue workers who lost their lives during 9-11. The quilt store owner had lost his twenty-seven year old daughter in the disaster. Barbara is a member of the United Federation of Teachers (UTF) quilting group. Barbara's husband, Gerry, was the photographer for all of the "QIN" kits donated to the two Staten Island Guilds.

"Mariner's Compass" by Jane Johnson. Jane Johnson was saddened by the loss of a new yacht club member who was enjoying being captain of his sailboat, with his wife and four children as crew. The new yacht club member was also very active in the local community and his church. He worked as an electrician for Cantor Fitzgerald, and was on the 104th floor of one of the World Trade Center towers when the first plane hit. He called home and told his son he was on his way ... but he never did come home. Jane wrote, "I attached an envelope to the back of this quilt, telling the many thoughts I had while making this quilt . I hope these thoughts guide them to a more comfortable feeling, and give them strength. I wrote, 'On 9-11, I was rotary-cutting my fabric for the UTF tessellation class sample. My son was in his office, which is next to the ground zero area. He did leave his building with his staff, and they ran through the dust, debris, and body parts, to the East River of lower Manhattan. My son's wife and I stayed near the phone for long hours waiting to hear he was all right. You must know I did cut all the fabric that day, and also started to put it together. Working with my hands, painting with fabric, was consoling ... the gray-white woven plaid background was the color of the sky over lower Manhattan for several days. It occurred when the firemen sprayed water on the burning buildings.'"

Jennifer Bowman, her son, and unborn child, received a log cabin quilt from her two former elementary school teachers, Helene Sokal and Lois Stehle. Jennifer's husband worked for Cantor Fitzgerald; they were in the process of building a home in New Jersey.

Helene and Lois wrote a personal note to their former student (a paraphrase of my words on pages 5 and 17).

2001

To Jennifer Bowman,

May the labor of our hands, Ease the grief in your heart.
Most Sincerely,
Helene Sokal, Lois Ste

On 9-11, Kathy Holler had been attending a conference in the Catskills in mid-New York state. Kathy was enjoying the magnificent view from her windows when she heard about the disaster. Her son was near the event and running for his life. She thought, "What conflict ... beauty from the window, versus family disaster." She started to work with some of her hand-dyed fabrics to soothe her emotions. She used the Broderie Perse method of appliqué for the cardinals and leaves. In this way, she remembers what is beautiful in her life, keeping this vision, and not dwelling on the disaster.

Primrose McVay was very touched by the idea behind the "QIN" kits, and paired one of the fabrics with her hand-dyed stash. The quilt was given to a fellow guild member who had previously taught her to appliqué. The fellow guild member was moving away, and had been deeply hurt by the disaster: Two men, whom she had cared for when they were young, lost their lives on 9-11.

The 9-11 Quilt Gallery   37

Carli Rose DeFillo, a sophomore student at New York University, created "World Without End" by appliquéing a 3-D white lily and small bunch of lily of the valley in the center with the "United We Stand" flag ribbon provided. Carli made the border of various blue "flaps" that flutter in the breeze, while the black border around the star signifies a mourning period. The quilt was given to Timothy Rice of the McCallum-Rice Funeral Home in Staten Island, who had helped so many families with memorial services for their loved ones.

Jane Johnson and the quilters of Staten Island delivered all of the finished quilts to the chosen families of the victims and said it was very emotional for all of them. The kinship among quilters unknown to each other has always been, and will continue to be, as strong a force as that between organ and blood donors and their recipients; strong as the men and women of the armed forces, the firemen and police officers from yesterday, today, forever, and always.

Barely six weeks after the September 11, 2001, terrorist attacks, 277 quilts in the "AMERICA: From The Heart" special exhibit were shown at the International Quilt Festival curated by director Karey Bresenhan in Houston, Texas. These quilts conveyed emotions ranging from outrage to impassioned patriotism. Many of the quiltmakers donated their quilts for auction—the proceeds of which were given to the Families of Freedom Scholarship Fund.™

Betty Nielsen of Fonda, Iowa, created the "Freedom Quilts" project a few short days after watching the initial reports of devastation in New York, Washington, D.C., and Pennsylvania. Her goal was to provide 4,000 quilts, one for each family of the victims. In mid-December, she and her husband, fellow organizer Pat Archer, and volunteer Beulah Emming went to New York City to deliver the 150 quilts made by her Varina, Iowa, quilting group – along with 1,350 others donated by individuals and guilds from all over the country and abroad. The quilts were transported by a donated Wal-Mart truck to a winter festival hosted by the city of New York for the victims' families. Kathleen Casey, sister of World Trade Center victim and police officer Eileen Mosca, took one of the quilts and sleeps with it every night. Betty also graciously delivered nineteen of my "QIN" quilt kits for any quilters among the surviving families.

Marty Frolli of Goleta, California, coordinator for the "Little Flags Quilt Project" created a small flag pattern available on the Internet with the resulting quilts to be given to the rescue workers and/or their families. She received 1,152 quilts, of which 412 went to every family and firehouse that lost a New York firefighter; 106 went to Pennsylvania firefighters, rescue workers, police, and volunteers in Shanksville and the surrounding communities; 140 were sent to families who lost a family member at the Pentagon, to those injured at the Pentagon and to the families of the anthrax victims; and 380 were sent to Washington, D.C., firemen, rescue workers, K-9 teams and hospital staff. The Little Flags Quilt Project committee in Santa Barbara, California, also sent 114 quilts to individuals around the country.

The American Quilters Society (AQS) of Paducah, Kentucky initiated the "Anchor Project" by collecting quilt blocks portraying hope and faith, having them assembled into quilts and then auctioning them during the AQS 2002 quilt show. The proceeds were donated to the New York Police and Fire Widows' and Children's Benefit Fund, NOVA (the National Organization for Victims Assistance), and the American Rescue Dog Association. The AQS also gave their authors the opportunity to have their own 9-11 quilts tour in their "United We Stand" exhibit. A book of the same name features some of these quilts, plus many from the Anchor Project. My own quilt, "What So Proudly We Hailed," featuring the Star Spangled Banner block with over 680 pieces, is included. Working on it allowed me to contemplate, and begin to understand, the gravity of the impact on the thousands of lives affected worldwide. The emotions I experienced resulted in images ranging from shock and fear, to pride, defiance, and the resolution to persevere. The quilt is infused with heart-wrenching symbolism. The star tips were cut off to represent the attack, then appliquéd back in place to represent the heroic efforts of the rescue teams and volunteers. The circular quilting depicts the radiating effects of Ground Zero on our world. Two severed but concentric half stars symbolize the steadfastness, tenacity, and courage our nation has shown in rebuilding, as

well as the efforts to help the victims' families, coworkers, and friends. Four doves represent the World Trade Center towers and airplane victims in New York, Pennsylvania, the Pentagon, and the lost fire and rescue teams in New York. A tearful eagle illustrates the grief of our country's citizens, while the Liberty Bell reminds us of our nation's strength.

Making quilts in response to historical events is not a new phenomenon. Individual quilters continue to express themselves in cloth as a response to events in their personal, local, and worldly lives. What is new in the last 15 years is the ability to instantly call for mass global volunteers through Internet e-mail groups, and radio and TV newscasts. Amy Leasure and Chris Davis could not have contacted the hundreds of quilters around the world to help with the World Trade Center Memorial Quilt without our modern technology. Tragically, Amy did not live to see the quilt panels displayed. She died of surgical complications on July 27, 2002. Many of us made a "Healing Quilt" for her recovery, which was then given to husband Michael and daughter Ashley. Among Amy's legacies is her task of honoring 9-11 victims in cloth—an act that gave hundreds of quiltmakers the opportunity to feel helpful, if only in bits of red, white, and blue cotton fabric ... and tiny stitches to mend our hearts.

"What So Proudly We Hailed," 2002; by author, in response to the tragedies of 9-11. Machine quilted by Cindy Hornet, Auxvasse, Missouri.

A Comparison of 19th and 20th Century Quilting Motivations

Carol Gebel, author of "Final Rite of Passage Quilts' in *Uncoverings 1995*, compares frontier women burying their children in quilts with the experiences of two 1980s women; Merry Nader, who wrapped her still-born child in its birth quilt, and Joyce a'Lora Neal, who buried her engaged daughter's wedding quilt with her after she and her fiance died in a car accident.[34]

Brenda Kirkpatrick made memorial quilts for her two sons, Terry and Rich, after their father Larry died in a professional car race on July 8, 1976. Brenda presented them with the quilts the following Christmas, possibly as a way to keep him alive another day. In the last block she embroidered, "Memory is the Treasurer and the Guardian of All Things."[35]

There are a couple of credible reasons why many modern Anglo-Americans have not commonly made and used casket or memorial quilts. After the Victorian era faded, talking about and planning elaborate funerals went out of fashion and became somewhat of a taboo subject. Instead of submerging ourselves in mourning dress and the accompanying memorial photos, samplers, trinkets, and household decor, we are now almost expected to quickly get on with our lives.[36] Many of us didn't grow up with these quiltmaking customs in our families, but many of our grandparents and great-grandparents did,

especially in the rural areas of early twentieth century America where distance or economic circumstances prevented them from hiring undertakers. It was common practice in some areas of the United States for the body of the deceased to be placed on a board, washed, and dressed for visiting mourners. Usually the kitchen door was laid over chairs and was called a "cooling board." A quilt was placed over the body until the men and boys of the household finished making the coffin for burial.[37] Even the motion picture industry portrayed historical frontier life with accuracy by depicting a woman's self-delivery and subsequent burial preparation when the infant later contracted whooping cough and died. His mother (played by actress Conchita Ferrell) washed him in a dish-pan and buried him in his christening gown wrapped in a quilt. When death was such an integral part of life, Americans were accustomed to seeing quilts as part of the traditional final journey.

The Role of the Quilt in Today's Final Journey Service

In discussing the role of quilts in funeral services and using them to ease the grieving process, I have interviewed funeral directors and talked with many people willing to relate their experiences. York Caskets of York, Pennsylvania, offers a "Countryside" casket lined with the Double Wedding Ring pattern adorning the head panel, overlay lining, throw (covering the lower half of the body) and on the pillow.

Babies of grieving parents are usually wrapped in blankets or baby quilts and are buried with them. Ruth Chaney of Mexico, Missouri, relates, "When my twin grandsons were born far too prematurely, we wrapped their tiny bodies in a white afghan I had made for their homecoming. I wished I'd known how to quilt then, because they would have been buried in quilts from their grandmother."

Dwight Schindler, of Arnold Funeral Home in Mexico, Missouri, says that funerals have become very personalized and it is almost the rule that surviving relatives display photos, memorials, and ephemeral objects of the deceased during the funeral and visitation periods. For my Dad's funeral, his golfing buddies had his golf bag filled with a floral arrangement for the visitation at the funeral home. The funeral industry itself has even designed caskets commemorating fans of cultural icons and hobbies such as caskets depicting tractors, angels, or Elvis Presley.

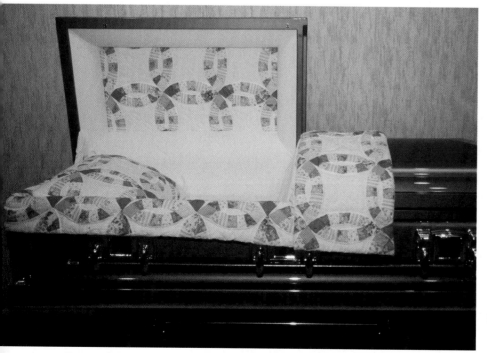

Countryside Casket by York Casket, York, Pennsylvania.

Top: "The Good Shepherd," by author. Bottom: "My Guardian Angel," by author. See pages 74 and 80 for projects.

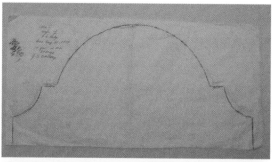

Upper left: Outline, rubbings, and resulting pattern of a decorative headstone. Bottom left: Myrna Raglin's rubbing of a headstone. Above: The results of the rubbing, interpreted in her finished quilt.

Quilters Prepare with Resolution and Humor

Myrna Raglin of California writes that she uses rubbings from tombstones in her appliqué work.

Since learning about casket quilts, she just may use them for her final journey quilt to be displayed at her funeral. She says the idea came from seeing a sample in a quilt shop in Sedona, Arizona, that included writing on each block with name, date, and place—but there didn't seem to be any relationships among the writings. She later learned the blocks were from rubbings on tombstones, and the writing was the name of the deceased along with the date and cemetery where it was done.

Teddy Pruett of Florida humorously wrote her own memorial verse in her quilt "Rotten Bones" to be displayed at her funeral "to bring a smile to my mourners' faces."

Teddy Pruett's "Rotten Bones" quilt.

Thursday Night Therapy's "All Through the Year" quilt, made by Ginny Berman, Bet Courey, Nancy Crippen, Carmen Crum, Bettie Jo Gibson, Marilyn Hood, Pat Menendez, Virginia Street, Dru Thomason, Karen Waechter, and Mary White.

Nancy Crippen of the "TNT" Thursday Night Therapy quilting group in Tampa, Florida, described the group's decision of how to share their group-made quilt. Members each chose a month to have the quilt in their home, but humorously solved the problem of who would eventually keep it. Nancy writes, "We had a lot of fun, giggles, and outright whoops of laughter that evening ... who would get to display it logically led to the next step (because most of us are in our sixties): Who will end up as the final owner. As members pass away, the quilt will be made available for display at their wake or memorial. (Urns may be placed on the member's block.) The last remaining member of the group retains the quilt. We had a great time laughing and joking about who would be the last one."

Marilyn Misner of Carson, Washington, related a humorous way of dealing with bequeathing her quilts after taking my class on commemorative memorial/casket quilts. "From time to time comments are made as to who will get which quilt from the remaining supply in Grandma's cupboards. One quilt in particular is the topic of their discussions as it is a large appliquéd beauty, which I made following the death of a son. I can't quite part with it as it holds many memories in its folds. The subject of death and burial doesn't really make good after-dinner conversation, although it is something we all think about as our 'young' bodies start to take on unique characteristics, but we just don't want to talk about it. Recently, we had a gathering of the clan. The day after a family wedding, two daughters, their husbands, and a son had all been sitting around the living room, laughing at some of the events of earlier years. The mood was upbeat, but one of the funny recollections had occurred following the death of a family member. This opened the door to the subjects of death and burial. Dad was sitting there, still trying to avoid the subject, when a son-in-law said, 'Yeah Mom, what do you and Dad want in the way of funeral arrangements? You know it's inevitable someday.' Seeing Dad's discomfort, I jokingly said, 'Oh, just take my appliqued quilt; it's the only one big enough to roll me up in and drop me in the hole.' Without hesitation and with a gleam in her eyes, my oldest daughter said, 'Mom, we may roll you up in it, but you can bet your bottom dollar that my fingers will have a tight grip on the corner of that quilt when you roll into that hole.' Well, that started the whole discussion and our wishes have been heard. Now my hope is to construct my own memorial quilt, small enough that my heirs may part with it for eternity. It will be beautiful ... a bit bright and 'glitzy,' like me. I've found the cutest little clown fabric that matches the red I've chosen for the roses in your Mourning Doves pattern. I'm going to finish my quilt and place it with the estate papers, along with instructions for its use. I'll get the last laugh! Maybe I can make one for my husband, with vegetables and his Kubota tractor on it. Life would surely be wasted without laughter."

Stitching to Soothe the Soul

During her father's lingering illness, Phyllis Miller of Murray, Kentucky, made a pillow for his casket from a quilted heart wall hanging she had previously used to teach quilting techniques. While her brothers made his casket, she added striped fabric on two sides so a bed pillow would fit into it. He was buried with her loving pillow under his head.

My mother, Emma Jean Giesler, wanted to give her sister, Marilyn Finson, a commemorative wall hanging as a memorial gift in honor of her husband Harry, who suddenly passed away in 2001. Marilyn knew of the forthcoming gift and brought several of his ties to be used in the piece. While she cut the ties and sewed them into

Phyllis Miller's teaching sample quilted heart pillow used as a casket pillow for her father. The casket was made by Miller's brothers.

"Don's Shirts" by Ruby Hale.

blocks, my mother recognized them and recalled those special occasions she and Dad were with Marilyn and Harry. The quilt gave solace to the maker—but as of this writing, it is still lost in the postal transit. Before embarking on a return trip with Aunt Marilyn to Hawaii to commemorate their first trip years ago with my father and uncle, Mom made a miniature crazy quilt from the left over scraps.

Ruby Hale of Martinsburg, Missouri, after seeing memorial quilts made with shirts from fellow guild member Sarah Maxwell's father-in-law, created "Don's Shirts" three months after his death.

She relates, "Every time I cut up a shirt, my thoughts were where we had been and what we had done when he had worn the shirt ... I tried to do the quilting and found it just too depressing and had it quilted by the Immaculate Conception Church Quilters. I'm glad I did it, but it was really difficult."

Jane Norman's "Mother's Quilt," 1999.

When her mother died, Jane Norman of Mexico, Missouri made a basket quilt during the last few weeks she was alive and named it "Mother's Quilt."

The one block that is pieced wrong represents the day her mother died. The rose border fabric was selected because roses were her favorite flowers. Jane said, "She was the only person I ever knew who could wear a white outfit to garden in and never get a bit of dirt on it." Before giving it to her father, she added a label on the

back that read, "In loving memory of Irene Long November 19, 1917 – August 23, 1999. These basket blocks were in progress at the time of her passing. May this quilt give you some comfort much the way she gave comfort to those around her ... Jane." Before her mother's death, Jane wanted to make something for each of her sisters. The fabrics used were from cocktail dresses and formals her mother made for herself and three daughters. Jane said, "I couldn't bring myself to cut up the dresses,

Scraps of the Long family's cocktail dresses were made into mini crazy quilts.

yet they were just hanging in the closet. So I bought a bottle of wine and a box of Kleenex. On a Friday night when I was alone, I drank wine, cried, and cut. It turned out to be good therapy and part of the healing." Jane made crazy quilt pillows and panels for all of them. There was a particular piece of voile that had been a favorite of her mothers' that she enjoyed touching each time Jane put the crazy quilt door panel on her mother's lap.

Lou Mongler, Mexico, Missouri, worked on a quilt started in a class with Marianne Fons while her brother was battling cancer.

She said the machine piecing allowed her to grieve and sew simultaneously. The finger, hand, and arm movements were repetitive and soothing, and as the quilt grew, she felt a sense of accomplishment in furthering its goal toward completion as well as her growing sense of inner peace and acceptance of her brother's untimely demise.

Barb Vlack's correspondence relates some of the same feelings: "I have made a couple of quilts that were not set up to do during a grieving process but ended up that way. I have found that events that occur during the making of a quilt become very much associated with that quilt. What might not have started out to be a funeral quilt might become one because that event occurred before the quilt was finished. I was making a Christmas quilt that definitely was not intended to be a funeral quilt but most of the piecing took place while I watched the funeral of Princess Di. I was greatly saddened by her sudden death, and I am glad I had this project to occupy me while I attended her funeral on TV. I was making my son's wedding quilt when John F. Kennedy, Jr. was killed, and felt glad I had that project to work on while I followed the events, again on TV. To counter that sadness, I

watched "You've Got Mail" incessantly because I love romantic comedies, especially with Meg Ryan and Tom Hanks. It was also cathartic, and the story reminded me how my son and his bride initially met through the Internet.

"Quilting brings a way to work through grief but also great joy. I quilted into the wedding quilt a lot of symbolism relating to the couple and the mission statement they wrote for their marriage. I used fabrics that had symbolism. I think we do the same for funeral quilts. We piece or quilt in little messages in one way or another as a memory statement. I do not feel that a funeral quilt has to be morbid. I would make one to celebrate life and probably find ways to present some humor in there, besides. Surely the dead or dying person had a few laughs. We need to cry, but we also need to sing and be happy about the person's life."

Scarlett Rose of California talked about funerals of guild members. At one, the deceased's favorite quilt was draped over her casket. At another, six of the guild member's last quilts were hung around the room.

Darlene Christopherson writes, "I want to have a headstone with appliqué patterns on it, so that I can perpetually be sharing with quilters."

Healing Journeys

Mourning, as defined in part in the fourth edition of *Funeral Customs the World Over* by Hamerstein and Lamers, is the process of helping to restore emotional balances after acute deprivation. It may involve rites, rituals, ceremonies, symbolic behavior, and significant customs.[38]

American quilters, seamstresses, and embroiderers have historically expressed their grief and healing

Lou Mongler's therapy quilt. Pattern by Liz Porter.

processes in cloth through casket, memorial, and mourn-ing quilts, and continue to do so. The custom of making and using these quilts is a healthy stress reducer, both physiologically and psychologically. Many years ago, a young female doctor who had been involved in cancer research was diagnosed with a very aggressive breast cancer. During one of her final treatment stays at Ellis Fischel Cancer Center in Columbia, Missouri, she said she now had the time to read all the books she had been putting off reading. In essence, she was preparing for her impending final journey and wanted to do something constructive and pleasurable. Quiltmakers can do this, and historically have done the same thing by preparing their own last quilt or casket quilt for a loved one to be draped over them or hung at their funerals. Some already

have prearranged funerals and have chosen Bible verses, music, and poems to be read. Though we cannot control when our final journeys take place, we can control how we want our final rite of passage to be carried out.

Another breast cancer victim, Ann Stamm Merrell, who passed away at the age of 47 in 1999, made "In the Space of Three Days, Everything Changed" to refer both to the time from Good Friday to Easter and to the three days from her biopsy to her diagnosis of cancer. She began its design while in the waiting room at the Stanford Breast Clinic, and finished the quilt after her first chemotherapy treatment. Also during her illness, she completed "The Blood of Christ: Adriamycin" in which she compares taking the caustic, red chemotherapy drug to taking Communion.[39]

A raffle quilt created by the Rainy Day Quilters of Ketchikan, Alaska, in 1998; the pattern was originally designed by Sheri Wilkinson Lalk. Raffle-winner Colleen Scanlon then donated this quilt to the Ketchikan City Council on Cancer Auction. Peggy Gelbrich, a member of the Rainy Day Quilters, had sewed quite a bit on this quilt. Peggy's husband, Ron, wanted to purchase the quilt since Peggy had spent so much time on it, and to commemorate their fortunate "benign" diagnosis in January 1999, when Peggy had a breast biopsy. The guild raised about $3,000, while the auction bidding finally ended at $7,000. The total auction receipts took in over $50,000 for local cancer patients to help with travel and medical expenses. Peggy said, "The quilt hangs in our bedroom. It is a reminder of many memories ... some scary, but mostly good."

Memorial verse and photo on the back of an Angel quilt dedicated to Peggy Kotek's sister, Patricia Pennyak.

Made in honor of her sister, Patricia Lea Wilson Pennyak, by Peggy Kotek, Minnesota. Peggy Kotek was on her way to New Jersey to see her sister, Patricia Lea Wilson Pennyak, when Patricia died. The Angel quilt was ready be to quilted, but Peggy had previously hand quilted one to wrap herself in "because I couldn't be there."

"Meredith's Tree of Life at Midnight," 1993. Commemorative, memorial and mourning quilt by author. I was working on the weeping willow border when my father, Frederick H. Giesler, died in 1993. I embroidered a bent rose under a willow, and wrote his vital statistics with a verse on the back. I then added all four of my grandparents' statistics on the reverse side under other willow trees.

"I Love You, Dad" memorial and mourning quilt was also made in 1993 to premier Elly Sienkiewicz's Baltimore Album fabrics. I turned her pattern inside out to show how my world had collapsed when Dad died.

"'Til Death Do Us Part" is a casket quilt made for my mother in preparation for her final journey. My father was a Nabisco salesman and their dog was named "Cookie." As in Victorian mourning pictures, the clock indicates the time the dearly beloved passed from this life.

A Comparison of 19th and 20th Century Quilting Motivations 53

"Family Weeping Willow Tree" is a casket memorial quilt designed to record family members' vital statistics between the branches, and is meant to be passed down within families.

I made "Mourning Doves" for me and my husband, with instructions that it should not be buried with the last one of us to survive the other, but is to be handed down in the family.

"I would also want to develop an attitude of celebration associated with a funeral quilt," said Barb Vlack (see page 48). "I would not want someone to feel eerie because someone died while using this quilt or because this quilt had been laid on the coffin of someone. I would want, instead, for this quilt to have achieved an honorable and revered status." I agree; I think Barb's statement is typical of quilters preparing their final journey quilt.

"Double Wedding Ring" casket quilt. On January 3, 1999, we learned that my husband's mother, Doretta Carlson, had made her final journey. I designed and handmade her casket quilt in three days.

Years ago, when Doretta first entered a nursing home, I made her a Seminole lap quilt to keep her warm, as she sat in a wheelchair most of the day. The least I could do was to wrap her casket in one last quilt for yesterday, today, forever, and always … and begin my healing journey once again.

I added a photo of Doretta and Fritz Carlson to the reverse of "Double Wedding Ring."

A Comparison of 19th and 20th Century Quilting Motivations   55

Crown of Thorns

15" x 45"

Quilt in photo to the left made by author, quilted by Cindy Horner, Auxvasse, Missouri.

Sewing Supplies:

Thread to match fabrics
Quilting thread
Pins
Fabric-marking pencil
14"-square freezer paper
Fabric and paper scissors
Optional: Large-eye needlepoint needle for trapunto in crown
3 yds. medium-weight yarn
Fine-point permanent marking pen (for writing a verse or personal information)

Fabric Supplies:

15-1/2" x 45-1/2" rectangle for background
18" x 48" batting
18" x 48" cotton backing material
2-1/4" x 125" bias strip of background fabric for a double-fold bias binding
14" square for crown of thorns
6"-square for cross
Optional: metallic quilting thread of your choice

Directions

1 See patterns on pages 94-95; 98. Trace crown onto dull side of freezer paper folded in half once. Cut out on lines. Iron shiny-side down onto 14" square fabric for crown. Trace around ironed paper with marking pen or pencil.

2 Remove paper and cut out a 1/8" seam allowance away from marked line inside and outside the crown.

3 Fold background fabric in half vertically across the 15" width to find the center. Center crown on background fabric and pin or loosely baste.

4 Needleturn the edges of the crown of thorns.

5 Optional: Draw three circles 1/4" apart in between the inside and outside edges of the thorns for two channels of trapunto. Use a small running stitch to create the channels. Thread the large-eye needlepoint needle with a 60" piece of yarn, tying ends together for double thickness. From the back, insert needle into the inside channel without poking through to the top crown fabric and exit about 2" to 3" (about the length of the needle) pulling the doubled yarn through. Reinsert the needle about 1/8" away from your exit point and again, exit 2" to 3" away. Go back to the first exit point and carefully snip the yarns apart. Continue in this manner to finish both channels. By doing this, the channels will lie flat.

6 Quilt as desired, or use 1" square or diagonal cross-hatching lines with metallic quilting thread. Bind.

Double Wedding Ring

15" x 45"

Sewing Supplies:

Thread to match fabrics
Quilting thread
Pins
Fabric-marking pencil
Fine-point Pigma pen
Template plastic
Fabric and paper scissors

Fabric Supplies:

15-1/2" x 45-1/2" white or cream cotton background fabric
2-1/4" x 125" bias strip of background fabric for a double-fold bias binding
18" x 48" batting
18" x 48" cotton backing fabric
12" square bright gold or silver for wedding rings
14" square gold for cross
Optional: Compass to draw quilting motifs of intersecting circles

Preparing templates and appliqué fabric

Quilting motif on page 93; patterns on pages 96-97. Trace appliqué patterns onto plastic template material and cut out. On the right side of the fabric, place templates, trace, and cut out leaving a scant 1/4" seam allowance around the entire traced line. This will be needle-turned under.

Directions

1 Fold the background in half vertically across the 15" width to find the center. Center cross A over the fold. Pin loosely to allow one bright gold or silver ring to go over and under each side. The left ring goes over the left side of the cross first. Refer to the photo for placement.

Hint: Have one needle threaded with thread matching the rings and one threaded to match the cross. Loosely baste all in place since you will need to be able to repin the appliqués away from the interlaced stitching of the rings over and under the cross.

2 Begin hand stitching the *left* edge of the left ring down first. Don't bury the knot when finished, just leave the needle in the work to be used later. With the other threaded needle, appliqué the left side of the cross then go back to stitching the right inside edge of the left ring where it touches the left inner corner of the cross. Continue down the right inside ring edge and stop just before the right outside edge of the right ring.

3 Appliqué the edge of the right ring under the right side of the cross and stop just before meeting the left ring.

4 Appliqué the right side of the cross finishing on the left side where you started.

5 Finish appliquéing the left half of the right ring, then the right half of the left ring.

6 Lightly mark the top with the suggested motif or quilt as desired. I chose the harp because my husband's father was a composer/conductor and his mother had a beautiful, alto voice that brought life to his solo and choir compositions.

7 Layer backing right-side down, batting, then top face up, and baste or pin together. Trim edges even and bind.

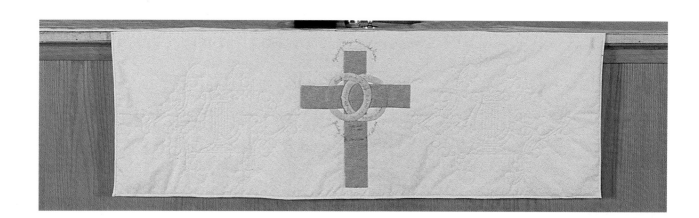

Family Weeping Willow Tree

15" x 45"

Sewing Supplies:

Thread to match fabrics
Quilting thread
Pins
Fabric-marking pencil
Fine-point brown Pigma pen
Freezer paper
Fabric and paper scissors

Fabric Supplies:

15-1/2" x 45-1/2"-long cream or light
    yellow cotton background fabric
2-1/4" x 125" bias strip of background
    color for double-fold bias binding
18" x 48" batting
18" x 48" cotton backing material
16" square dark green for willow tree
3" diameter circle for red rose
5" square medium green for rose stem
    and leaves

Directions

1 See patterns and motifs on pages 94-95, 99, 100-101. Trace tree onto dull size of freezer paper folded in half once. Cut out on the lines. Iron shiny-side down, onto right side of 16" square fabric for tree. Trace around ironed paper with marking pen or pencil.

2 Remove paper and cut out 1/8" seam allowance away from marked line. Repeat process for rose stem and leaves, omitting centerfold in freezer paper and using the 5" square medium green fabric.

3 Fold the background fabric in half vertically across the 15" width to find the center. Center and temporarily pin the willow tree A over the fold. Loosely baste in place and remove pins to avoid catching your sewing thread.

4 Place and pin rose stem B at the base of tree. Tuck in leaves C under the stem. Appliqué leaves first, then the step, stopping at stem/calyx junction to insert folded rose bud D. (See figures A through D.)

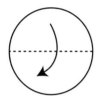

Fig. A: Fold rosebud in half.

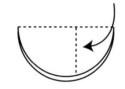

Fig. B: Fold right side almost to center.

Fig. C: Fold left side almost to center.

Fig. D: Gather using double thread to secure.

5 Make rose bud; insert into calyx. Finish dewing down calyx and stem. Secure top of rose bud to the background fabric.

6 Using the permanent Pigma pen, write your family history between the willow branches.

7 Suggested quilting motifs are Eternal Flames of Love and Guiding Star. Mark top, then baste top, batting, and backing together.

8 Outline-quilt all appliquéd pieces before quilting as desired. Trim edges and bind.

Floral Silhouette

15" x 45"

Sewing Supplies:

Thread to match fabrics
Quilting thread
Pins
Needle
Fabric-marking pencil
Freezer paper
Fabric and paper scissors

Fabric Supplies:

15-1/2" x 45-1/2" long white-on-white
 print background

2-1/4" x 125" bias strip of background
 color for double-fold bias binding
18" x 48" batting
18" x 48" cotton backing material
12" square solid or black-on-black print
 for silhouette
15" wide x 30" long green print for vine
 wreath
4 or more stiff or soft wired-edge
 ribbons 1" to 2" wide x 36" long
 (grosgrain is not recommended)
Several assorted 3" circles cotton for
 assorted folded roses
Optional: metallic thread for quilting;
 125" decorative cording or ribbon
 with 3-D rosettes

Preparing templates and appliqué fabric

See patterns on pages 125 and 126. Trace appliqué patterns onto dull non-waxy side of freezer paper and cut out. On the right side of the fabric, place freezer paper templates; trace and cut out, leaving a scant 1/4" seam allowance around the entire traced line. This will be needle-turned under.

Directions

1 For the silhouette, cut a 12" square solid black or black-on-black cotton print.

2 Tape a 12" square piece of freezer paper to a wall and have your subject sit sideways as close as possible to it. Put a floor lamp in front of the subject to cast a head and neck profile shadow onto the freezer paper.

3 With a marker on the dull, non-waxy side of the freezer paper, trace the subject's head and neck profile, making sure there is enough room for a scant 1/4" seam allowance.

4 Cut out the marked silhouette freezer paper pattern. Trace onto the black fabric and cut out a scant 1/4" away from the marked silhouette. Center it onto the 15-1/2" x 45-1/2" background fabric and appliqué down.

5 Because all silhouette profiles are of various shapes and sizes, trace the vine wreath onto the freezer paper in the same manner as the silhouette, then lay it over the appliquéd profile to see if any of the leaves need to be adjusted around the facial features. Cut back any leaf that is too close. (See photo.) When satisfied with the vine wreath placement around the silhouette, cut out the adjusted freezer paper pattern.

6 Iron, waxed-side down, onto the vine wreath fabric and trace with a fabric safe marker. Cut a scant 1/4" away from the traced line.

7 Pin or baste in place around the silhouette and appliqué.

8 Make as many ribbon and folded roses as desired and tack onto the quilt. For Large

Ribbon Roses: Cut a 24"- to 36"-long x 1"- to 2"-wide ribbon. (For smaller roses, use 18"- to 24"-long x 1/2"- to 1"-wide ribbons.) Using 24"-long matching, doubled thread, sew a running gathering stitch down the middle of the ribbon from end to end, folding the raw ends in. With the same needle, gather about half of the ribbon. Start turning the gathered end of the ribbon toward the opposite, ungathered end to form a rosette, taking stitches to hold it in place where needed. Continue gathering and stitching until the end of the ribbon can be tucked and tacked down behind the rose. Attach to quilt top with tacking stitches from the quilt back. For Folded Roses: Cut several 2" to 3" circles from different fabrics, two for each rose. With right sides together, sew 1/8" from raw edges, leaving an opening to turn right side out. Turn and stitch opening closed. See figures A through D to create buds from these:

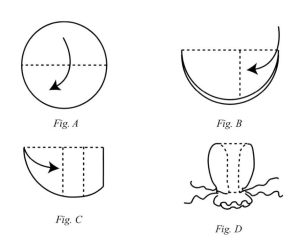

Fig. A

Fig. B

Fig. C

Fig. D

Make buds and tack onto quilt as desired Add pearl and sparkling beads if desired to gathered area.

9 For beaded berries, trace a penny onto the right side of berry fabrics. Cut out a scant 1/4" away for seam allowance. Baste 1/8" away from raw edges with doubled thread for gathering. Cut small amounts of quilt batting for stuffing berries. Place batting inside berries; gather tightly and sew closed. With thread matching the bead color, pierce the berry from the gathered bottom with the double threaded needle through to the top, then add the bead. Holding the bead in place, squash the berry between your fingers to flatten it a bit, then insert the needle back into the bead, pulling the thread all the way through to the gathered bottom. Knot the thread in the bottom of the berry. Tack in place onto the quilt.

10 Suggested quilting motifs are to draw more branches and leaves starting at the bottom of the neck and extending outward on both sides of the silhouette's head. Using metallic quilting thread makes them beautifully visible. Use a different metallic thread for the branches and leaves drawn on the head or outline quilt motifs if a printed fabric was used. See photo for ideas.

11 Mark top, then baste top, batting, and backing together. Trim edges even, quilt and bind. Attaching decorative cording to quilt just inside the front binding is optional. Use couching stitches with matching or nylon thread. Use the permanent marking pen to ink in the name and date if desired.

Floral Cross

24" square

Quilt in photo to the left made by author, quilted by Cindy Horner, Auxvasse, Missouri.

Sewing Supplies:

Thread to match fabrics
Quilting thread
Pins
Needle
Fabric-marking pencil
14" square freezer paper
Fabric and paper scissors

Fabric Supplies:

24-1/2" square cotton background fabric
*Strips to equal 2-1/2" wide by 100" long background fabric for binding if making one finished block.
*28" square cotton backing and batting
14" square white cotton print for cross
12" square red print for folded roses
1-1/2" x 45" length of ribbon (use a sheer ribbon with wires on both sides or satin ribbon)

Note: This may be used as one block among others or as a finished piece by itself. Use yardages with stars for one block finished piece.

Directions

1 On freezer paper with ruler and pencil, draw a cross 2" thick by 10" wide by 12" tall. Trace cross onto the dull side of the freezer paper and cut out on lines. Iron onto fabric, shiny-side down. Trace around with fabric marker.

2 Cut 1/8" away from drawn lines.

3 Fold 24-1/2" background fabric in half twice to find center. Center cross, and pin. Needle turn appliqué in place.

4 Make five folded roses, as shown in Figures A through E. From 12" square red fabric, cut five 2" x 4" rectangles. Fold down top edge 1/4". Fold left side to center, forming a triangle. Fold right side over to within 1/8" of left fold. With doubled matching thread, baste bottom raw edges, pulling threads tightly to form bud. Secure.

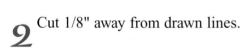

Fig. A   *Fig. B*

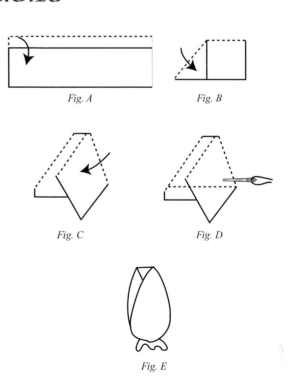

Fig. C   *Fig. D*

Fig. E

5 Make five small dots on edge of ribbon every 9", totaling five dots. Tie a small knot at each end of the ribbon to prevent fraying. Loosely tie one knot at each 9" interval dot. These become the sepal and calyx for the buds.

6 With thread to match the ribbon, baste five loose knots side by side, allowing loose ribbon in between each knot to loop. (See photo.)

Position on cross and pin. Insert five folded buds and appliqué in place. Secure ribbon in place.

7 Sandwich backing (right side down), batting and block (right side up) and baste or pin. Quilt and bind.

'Til Death Do Us Part

15" x 45"

Sewing Supplies:

Thread to match fabrics
Quilting thread
Paper and fabric scissors
Pins
Template plastic
Fabric marker
Fine-point Pigma pen
Compass for drawing arcs
Other: Photo transfer paper (check local
    copy businesses)

Fabric Supplies:

15-1/2" x 45-1/2" background fabric
18" x 48" batting
18" x 48" cotton backing material
2-1/4" x 125" bias strip of background
    fabric for a double bias binding
12" square UNWASHED white muslin for
    photo transfer
(2) 1" x 27" strips of two different colors
    for wreath
(3) or more 5" square scraps of assorted
    floral color
(4) or more 5" square scraps for leaves

Preparing templates and appliqué fabric

Trace appliqué patterns (page 71) onto plastic template material and cut out. On the right side of the fabric, place templates, trace, and cut out, leaving a scant 1/4" seam allowance around the entire traced line. This will be needle-turned under.

Directions

1 Take a 5" x 7" photo (or have a smaller one enlarged to that size) with the special photo transfer paper to a copy center that has a color laser copier. The machine needs to be set to REVERSE the photo image onto the transfer paper since you afterwards need to heat transfer it to the unwashed white muslin fabric. For best results, go to a store that has a commercial heating press for transferring T-shirt images. You can do this with a dry iron at home pre-heated at its hottest setting for 10 minutes. Iron the muslin first so there are no wrinkles and brush away any lint to avoid white specks in the finished photo. While the fabric is warm, position the photo, paper face down, onto the center of the fabric. Press with a grinding motion for at least 30 seconds without letting any area cool. Gently turn back one corner to see if the image has transferred. If not, repeat ironing. Once the color has transferred, in one motion, peel the paper from the fabric.

2 Fold and finger press the background fabric in half, making sure there is a 1/4" seam allowance on the muslin photo. (Note: Your photo may allow a full circle without making the sides straight. I wanted my parents' wedding rings to show and a full circle wouldn't suffice.)

3 Cut out the background fabric 1/4" INSIDE the marked area to reveal the photo. Needle-turn appliqué the edges to the photo.

4 To prepare the two 1" x 27" wreath strips, fold and iron a scant 1/4" under on each long raw edge so they barely meet in the center. See Fig. A:

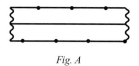

Fig. A

5 Loosely baste together in a zigzag fashion. See Fig. B:

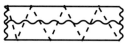

Fig. B

6 Lay and temporarily pin one prepared wreaths trip around the photo wrong side down. Interlace and pin the other strip with the first one. When satisfied with the positioning, loosely baste, then appliqué in place.

There are several photo transfer papers on the market now. Be sure to carefully read the directions for fabric preparation as well as the suggestions for suitable color copiers. I used "New" Motif Heat Transfer Paper, which recommended the following laser color copiers: Canon-200, 300, 350, 500, 550, 700, 800, 1000; Kodak: 1525, 1525 plus, 1550, 1550 plus, 1560, 1565; Minolta: CF70, CF80, CF900; Mita: 7500; Scitex-Spontane: Ricoh-NC5006, 5106, 5206, 8115, 305, 2003, 2103, 2203; Xerox-Majestik, Regal, Empress, DocuColor 40; Sharp-AR-C860, AR-C860, AR-C861/862; Toshiba-FC-70; Savin-SDC206/206E. Note: DO NOT pre-wash the 12" square muslin for the photo transfer.

7 Make as many leaves and flowers as you want. (The number will vary according to your choice of background fabric.) Place them where they do not detract from the photo. Appliqué in place. See Figs. C through F for bud construction.

8 Lightly mark the top with quilting designs as desired, or use the circle included in the pattern section. Start marking on either side of the photo so the interlocking circle design will be centered.

9 Trim edges even and bind. Sign and mark quilt with loved ones' vital statistics on the back or front as desired.

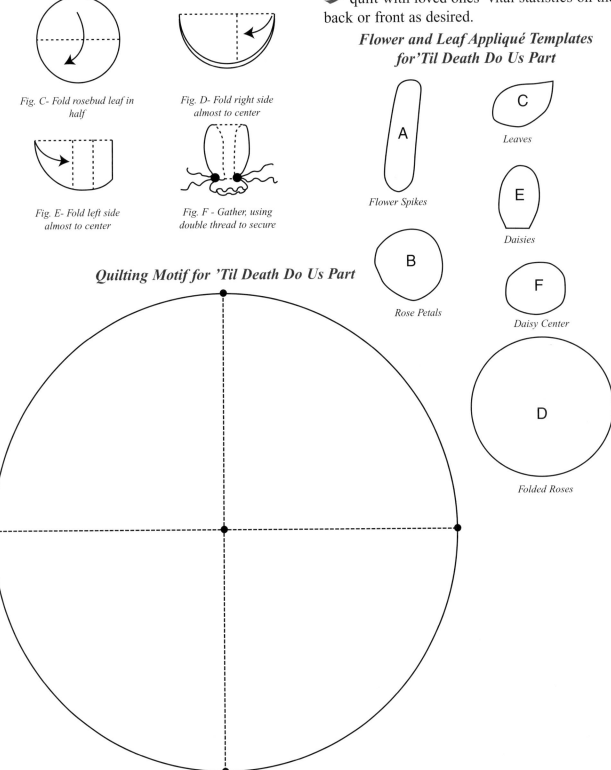

Fig. C- Fold rosebud leaf in half

Fig. D- Fold right side almost to center

Fig. E- Fold left side almost to center

Fig. F - Gather, using double thread to secure

Flower and Leaf Appliqué Templates for 'Til Death Do Us Part

A
Flower Spikes

C
Leaves

E
Daisies

B
Rose Petals

F
Daisy Center

D
Folded Roses

Quilting Motif for 'Til Death Do Us Part

Dots indicate circle intersection points.

Flying Angels

24" block

Quilt in photo to the left made by Mary Oberhaus, Vandalia, Missouri.

Sewing Supplies:

Thread to match fabrics
Quilting thread
Pins
Needle
Fabric marking pencil
Freezer paper
Fabric and paper scissors
2 sheets 8-1/2" x 11" paper

Fabric Supplies:

26" square batting
26" square backing
24-1/2"square cotton background
14" square white-on-white print for angel
2" by 100" strip bias background fabric for binding

Directions

1 See patterns and motifs on pages 102, 106, and 107. Trace appliqué angel pattern onto the dull side of the freezer paper. Iron on right side of fabric. Trace with a fabric marker. Remove the paper and cut a healthy 1/8" away from the drawn lines.

2 Fold background fabric in half twice to find the center. Center and pin angel. Appliqué in place.

3 To transfer flying angel quilting designs, trace onto a piece of paper, then reverse and trace the motif on another piece of paper. Tape the pattern to a window or a glass coffee table with a light source underneath. Tape appliquéd block onto the glass, placing the angel diagonally in the top right corner. Trace lightly with a non-permanent fabric marker. Reposition the block reversing the flying angel motifs as needed to complete the quilting lines. Draw diagonal 1" lines behind the flying angels at a 45-degree angle, or draw random squiggly curls.

4 Sandwich backing (right side down), batting, and block (right side up), and baste or pin. Quilt and bind.

The Good Shepherd

14" x 45"

Sewing Supplies:

Thread to match fabrics
Quilting thread
Pins
Needle
Fabric marking pencil
Freezer paper
Fabric and paper scissors
Fine-point brown Pigma permanent marking pen

Fabric Supplies:

15-1/2" x 45-1/2" long sky-color cotton background fabric

2-1/4" x 125" bias strip of background color for double-fold bias binding
18" x 48" batting
18" x 48" cotton backing material
6" x 12" white print for robe
3" x 9" dark blue strips for robe vestments
4" square for dark blue hood
4" square flesh-color print for head and hands
15" square white or cream print for (3) sheep
6" square black for sheep faces and legs
1" x 12" brown strip for shepherd's staff

Preparing templates and appliqué fabric

See patterns and motifs on pages 101, 103-105. Trace appliqué patterns separately onto the dull side of the freezer paper and cut out. Iron, shiny-side down, onto the right side of the appropriate appliqué fabrics. Trace around all templates, then cut a healthy 1/8" away from the drawn lines. This seam allowance will be needle-turned under. Peel off paper and trace any inked features on the fabric pieces now.

Directions

1 Fold the background in half vertically across the 15" width to find the center. Center and pin robe A over the fold.

2 Place and pin the hands D and D reverse (rv) under the sleeves. Needle-turn appliqué hands in place, but leave the shepherd's left thumb area open until pinning staff L in place. Tuck in the seam allowance on the staff under the shepherd's left hand before you finish appliquéing the thumb area.

3 Appliqué the robe in place.

4 Pin and sew the vestments B and C on top of the robe.

5 Transfer and trace the shepherd's facial features to face F with the Pigma pen. Referring to photo, pin and sew in place on hood E.

6 Place and pin the three sheep, G, I, and K, around the shepherd. Pin their corresponding faces, H, J, and L under their bodies. On sheep K, tuck in legs M and N, and appliqué down before sewing its body, K. Appliqué the faces first, then the bodies.

7 Mark the top using suggested quilting motif, or as desired. Halo around the shepherd is a part of the haloed cross motif. Freehand drawn clouds can also be added around the perimeter of the quilt if desired.

8 Baste top, batting, and backing together.

9 Outline the quilt around all appliquéd pieces, then quilt, trim edges, and bind.

Heavenly Harp

20" x 20" wholecloth quilt

Quilt in photo to the left made by Carolyn McBride, Vandalia, Missouri.

Sewing Supplies:

1 or 2 metallic or cotton quilting threads, fabric scissors, ruler, and fabric marker

Fabric Supplies:

20-1/2" x 20-1/2" square cotton background

Bias strips of background fabric to equal 2-1/4" x 85" long for binding

22" square batting

22" square cotton backing fabric

Directions

1 See pattern on pages 108-111. Center and trace half of harp pattern onto a 16" square paper with a dark marker. Flip pattern to draw other half.

2 Use a light table or window to center fabric over pattern. Lightly trace whole harp onto fabric

3 Layer backing (right side down), batting, and traced top. Baste together.

4 Quilt the harp with a metallic thread for a glittering effect first then quilt the background in cross-hatching lines 1" apart in another color.

5 Bind.

Mourning Doves

14" x 45"

Sewing Supplies:

Thread to match fabrics
Quilting thread
Pins
Needle
Fabric marking pencil
Freezer paper, 18" wide
Fabric and paper scissors
Fine-point Pigma permanent marking pen

Fabric Supplies:

15-1/2" x 45-1/2" white or cream print cotton background fabric
2-1/4" x 125" bias strip of background color for double-fold bias binding
18" x 48" batting
18" x 48" cotton backing material
18" square medium to dark green for rosebud wreath
12" square beige or gray print for two doves
4" x 5" yellow or gold solid for cross
15" square red print for rosebuds
(4) 1-1/2" x 12" strips red print for ruched roses

Preparing templates and appliqué fabric

See patterns and motifs on pages 106, 112-115. Trace appliqué patterns onto the dull side of the freezer paper adding the B and B reverse (rv) bud branches to wreath A before cutting out on the lines. After cutting out the freezer paper templates, iron shiny-side down onto the right side of the appropriate appliqué fabrics. Trace around all templates, then cut a healthy 1/8" away from the drawn lines. This seam allowance will be needle-turned under. Peel off

Directions

1 Finger press the background in half vertically across the 15" width to find the center. Center and pin rosebud wreath A over the fold. Loosely baste the wreath and remove pins to allow for easier sewing.

2 Referring to photo, locate rosebuds tucked beneath or on top of the leaves. Use the pattern for the appropriate bud branch to cut slightly smaller buds from the red print fabric. Appliqué the buds beneath the leaves first. Pin the buds on top of the other appropriate leaves for now.

3 Appliqué the green wreath next.

4 Locate rosebuds under the cross and on the bottom branch that were reverse appliqués in the photo. Cut approximately 1/2" to 3/4" down the center of the green leaf, being careful not to cut the background fabric.

5 Insert red fabric slightly smaller than the leaf. Needle-turn under the raw edges of the green leaf over the red fabric and appliqué through all the layers.

6 Finally, appliqué the remaining rosebuds over the rest of the green leaves, referring to the photo for placement.

7 Appliqué the cross in place, then the doves.

8 Join the four 1-1/2" x 12" strips together lengthwise. Turn and press under both long edges to meet down the center.

9 On right side along one long edge, mark 1" dots. On bottom edge, offset the dots by 1/2" in a zigzag fashion. (See fig. A.)

10 Using 48" of matching double thread, use small basting stitches to connect the dots from the bottom to the top. Tie a knot at the end to secure. (See fig. B.)

11 When evenly tight, cut into three sections and secure ends to prevent unraveling. Referring to photo, place one section's end to wreath and tack down. Continue tacking in a circular motion to secure rose edges, going around once. Use the rest of the ruching to form a small circle in the center of the rose, tacking on top of previous circle. Secure in center. Continue in the same manner for remaining ruched roses.

12 Ink loved one's vital statistics within the wreath before marking quilting motifs. Mark using suggested quilting motifs, or as desired.

13 Baste top, batting, and backing together.

14 Outline quilt around all appliquéd pieces, then quilt, trim edges, and bind.

My Guardian Angel

15" x 45"

Sewing Supplies:

Thread to match fabrics
Quilting thread
Pins
Needle
Fabric marking pencil
Freezer paper, 18" wide
Fabric and paper scissors
Fine-point brown Pigma permanent marking pen

Fabric Supplies:

15-1/2" x 45-1/2" pink cotton background fabric
2-1/4" x 125" bias strip of background color for double-fold bias binding
18" x 48" batting
18" x 48" cotton backing material
18" square white print for angel and wings
3-1/2" x 9" light blue for pinafore
4" square flesh color for face and hands
2-1/2" square gold print for halo
5" square cream print for lamb

Directions

1 See patterns and motifs on pages 116-118. Trace angel parts separately onto dull side of freezer paper. Cut out on lines. Iron, shiny-side down onto right side of appropriate fabrics for entire angel. Trace around ironed papers with marking pen or pencil.

2 Remove paper and cut out a healthy 1/8" seam allowance away from marked line. Repeat process for all angel parts.

3 Fold the background fabric in half vertically across the 15" width to find the center. Center and temporarily pin the dress robe A over the fold. Loosely baste in place and remove pins to avoid catching your sewing thread.

4 Place and pin wings E and E reverse (rv) under dress robe, referring to the photo. Appliqué.

5 Tuck halo D under hood of dress robe and sew in place.

6 Appliqué dress robe.

7 Place and pin robe pinafore F over dress robe. Tuck hands B and B (rv) in place and appliqué robe pinafore before sewing hands on.

8 Trace facial features on the angel's face C with Pigma pen. Appliqué in place, then add more inked hair around angel's face and hood.

9 Pin and appliqué lamb close to angel. Add facial features and curly wool ringlets with Pigma pen.

10 Mark suggested heart and lamb quilting motifs or mark as desired.

11 Mark and baste top, batting, and backing together.

12 Outline quilt all the appliquéd pieces to make them stand out from the background.

13 Quilt, trim edges, and bind.

Peace Dove on Olive Branch

(Quilting Lines or Appliqué Motifs)
10" x 7-1/2"

Quilt in photo to the left made by author and quilted by Cindy Horner, Auxvasse, Missouri.

Sewing Supplies for Quilted Dove and Olive Branch:

Quilting thread that will show up on the background material
Fabric marker
Ruler

Fabric Supplies for Quilted Dove and Olive Branch:

20-1/2" square cotton background
22" square batting
22" square cotton backing
Bias strips to equal 2-12" wide x 85" long cotton fabric for binding

Sewing Supplies for Appliquéd Dove and Olive Branch:

Thread to match fabrics
Quilting thread
Pins
Needle
Ruler
Fabric marking pencil

Freezer paper
Fabric and paper scissors
Black embroidery floss for eye
Embroidery needle
Fine point Pigma permanent marking pen

Fabric Supplies for Appliquéd Dove and Olive Branch:

20-1/2" square cotton background (gold- or silver-edged print or plain satin is lovely)
22" square batting
22" square cotton backing material
1" square yellow for dove beak
6" square white or cream print for dove body
3-1/2" square white or cream print for largest wing feather
3" square scrap white or cream print for medium wing feather
2" square scrap white or cream print for small wing feather
4 assorted scrap white or cream prints for four 4-1/2" long tail feathers
8" square green or brown print for olive branch

Quilting Directions

1 See patterns and motifs on pages 114, 115, 119. For quilting: Tape dove pattern to a window or a glass coffee table with a light source underneath. Tape background fabric onto the glass, placing the dove 6" down from the top center, and trace lightly with a fabric marker. Remove dove pattern without disturbing the background fabric.

2 Tape olive branch pattern in the same manner underneath the fabric. Align the branch under the dove, matching the dots. Trace the olive branch.

3 Using a ruler, draw vertical lines 1/2" apart from top to bottom behind the dove, starting in the center of the block so they will be centered. Continue drawing lines through the rest of the block.

4 Sandwich backing (right side down), batting, and background fabric (right side up), and baste or pin. Put in frame and quilt.

Appliqué Directions

1 Trace and label pattern pieces onto the dull side of the freezer paper as follows: Dove body (A); dove beak (B); large wing feather (C); medium wing feather (D), small wing feather (E); first tail feather (aligned with Dove back), (F); fattest tail feather, (G); longest tail feather, (H); and smaller tail feathers (I).

2 Cut out on the lines. Pin on right sides of fabrics shiny-side down and iron. Trace around patterns and remove paper. Cut a healthy 1/8" away from the drawn lines. Mark eye on dove body for embroidery later.

3 6" down from the background center top, place dove body and pin. Place and pin tail feathers according to photo starting with F. Appliqué.

4 Pin and appliqué dove beak B.

5 Pin wing feathers in place according to the photo, starting with large wing C. Appliqué in place; C, D, and then E. Using three strands of black embroidery floss, embroider dove's eye, using satin stitches.

6 Outline quilt around dove and olive branch twice with 1/8" lines. The first lines should be right next to the appliqués and the second set 1/8" away.

7 Finish in the same manner as in step 4 of the quilting directions.

Remembrance Bouquet

15" x 36"

Quilt, above, made by Susan Masulit, Vandalia, Missouri.

Sewing Supplies:

Thread to match fabrics
Quilting thread
Pins
Needle
Fabric-marking pencil
Plastic template material
Fabric and paper scissors
Optional: 1/2" bias bar

Fabric Supplies:

15-1/2" x 36-1/2" cotton background fabric
2-1/4" x 150" bias strip of background color for double-fold bias binding
18" x 36" batting
18" x 36" cotton backing material
18" square cotton for bow
18" square for stems and bud branches
Assorted flowers and leaves cut from cotton fabric for Broderie Perse appliqué
Assorted 1" x 12" strips green for stems
Optional: Scrap 3" diameter circles for folded flower buds

Directions

1 See patterns on pages 120-122. Label and trace bud branches onto template plastic. Cut out and trace around them on RIGHT side of fabric. Cut out with a healthy 1/8" seam allowance. Label and trace top and bottom bow edge A and C, bow ties D, and bow knot E onto template plastic. Cut out and trace as before.

2 See illustration of bow and notice how the right bow body B is top over bottom and left over right side flipped from the left bow body. Label and trace the LEFT BOW BODY B first onto template plastic. Cut out and trace around on right side of fabric as in step 1. To make RIGHT half of bow body, use the same template, but turn the top of it over the bottom, then flip left side over right. Trace on the right side of the fabric, and cut it out with a 1/8" seam allowance.

3 On LEFT bow body B, match, pin, and sew the top left of bow edge A. Match, pin, and sew left bottom bow edge C to the left bow body B. Continue in the same manner for the RIGHT bow body B.

4 Fold background fabric in half vertically across the 15" width to find the center. Center and pin Bow Knot E 6" down from the top center edge.

5 Insert sewn LEFT and RIGHT bow body Bs under the match marks to Bow Knot E. Pin temporarily. Insert and pin bow ties D under the bottom of the bow knot, matching marks.

6 As seen in photo, insert and pin bud branches.

7 To make bouquet stems, cut several 1" by 12" pieces of fabric. With WRONG sides together, sew a 1/4" seam down the length of the stem. At the ironing board, manipulate the seam to the center of the stem. Insert bias bar and iron.

8 Appliqué stems in place under the bow ties D and under bow bodies. Needle-turn appliqué the bud branches leaving open those areas you wish to insert flowers and buds.

8a. Optional Folded Flowers:

Cut 3" diameter circles. Fold in half. Fold left side towards center, then fold right side on top about 1/4" from left folded edge. Baste bottom raw edges with doubled thread pulling to gather into a bud shape. Secure gathering threads. Insert under bud branches as desired and appliqué. (See figs. A – E.)

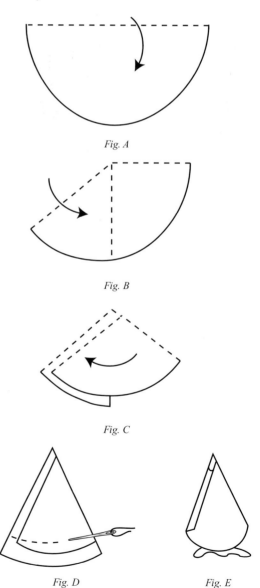

Fig. A

Fig. B

Fig. C

Fig. D   *Fig. E*

9 Cut a short stem(s) and insert under the top of bow knot E. Appliqué stem in place, then appliqué cut flowers and leaves.

10 Appliqué left and right bow bodies in place, then bow knot E over them.

11 Pin and appliqué cut flowers and buds as desired.

12 Sandwich backing (right side down), batting and block (right side up) and baste or pin.

13 Quilt around bouquet close to each motif. Mark and quilt the rest of the background as desired. Quilt and bind.

Star of David and Menorah Trees

15" x 45"

(Menorah Trees & Star of David appliqué may also be used as a quilting motif)

Quilt in photo to the left made by author and quilted by Cindy Horner, Auxvasse, Missouri.

Sewing Supplies:

Thread to match fabrics
Quilting thread
Paper and fabric scissors
Pins
Freezer paper
Fabric marker

Fabric Supplies:

15-1/2" x 45-1/2" long cotton background fabric
18" x 48" batting
18 x 48" cotton backing material
2-1/4" x 125" bias strip of background fabric for a double bias binding
12" squares for Star of David
(2) 12" squares for Menorah trees
12" square for 18 candles

Directions

1 See patterns on pages 123, 124. Trace star pattern onto the dull side of a 12" square of freezer paper with a vertical fold down the center. Cut out on the lines.

2 Iron onto a 12" square. Trace around outside and inside of triangle star. Cut out a healthy 1/8" away from all drawn lines. Repeat with remaining Star of David fabric square.

3 Trace Menorah tree pattern onto an unfolded freezer paper in the same manner as for the star. Iron, trace, and cut out as above.

4 Repeat same process for the candles.

5 Fold 15-1/2" x 45-1/2" background fabric in half twice to find the center. Center one star triangle over the center, pin, and need-turn appliqué in place. Center the remaining star triangle upside down and right side up over the first triangle and appliqué in place.

6 Center, place, and pin the Menorah trees on both sides of the star. Needle-turn appliqué in place. Center the remaining star triangle upside down and right side up over the first triangle and appliqué in place.

7 Center, place, and pin the Menorah trees on both sides of the star. Needle-turn appliqué the trees in place, leaving an opening at the top of each branch to insert the candles later.

8 Insert candles into branches and appliqué in place.

9 Mark and quilt as desired. Bind.

White Roses

35" square

Quilt in photo to the left made by author, and quilted by Cindy Horner, Auxvasse, Missouri.

Sewing Supplies:

Thread to match fabrics
Quilting thread
Paper and fabric scissors
Ruler
Pins
Optional: 1/4" wide or 1/2" wide bias
    Freezer paper for optional leaves
Fabric marker

Fabric Supplies:

35-1/2" square cotton for background
Bias strips of background fabric to equal
    2-1/4" wide x 175" long for double-
    fold bias binding
5 large flowers cut from a floral fabric
    (generally 1 yard)
Optional: Cut 3 or more leaf motifs from
    the same fabric
1" x 21" long bias strips of green for
    flower stems
Optional: Green scraps for 4 or more
    leaves if not using leaves from floral
    fabric
38" square each of batting and cotton
    backing

Directions

1. Cut five flowers and optional leaves from the floral fabric, adding a healthy 1/8" seam allowance. See photo for placement on background block and pin.

2. To make bouquet stems, cut (5) 1" x 21" pieces of fabric. With wrong sides together, sew a 1/4" seam down the length of the stem. At the ironing board, manipulate the seam to the center of the stem. Insert bias bar and iron.

Option: If you are using scraps to make leaves, trace leaf onto the dull side of the freezer paper and cut out (see patterns on page 98). Lay on right side of fabric, shiny-side down, and iron. Trace with a fabric marker. Remove paper and cut out with a healthy 1/8" seam allowance.

3. Insert stems and leaves under flowers and loosely baste in place. Needle-turn under the edges of the leaves and appliqué in place. Sew stems, then appliqué flowers in place over the stems.

4. Sandwich backing (right-side down), batting, and block (right side up), and baste or pin. Quilt as desired and bind.

Quilting Motifs

Star of Bethlehem

12" square for quilting

Directions

1 See page 107 for pattern. Trace star pattern onto paper with a dark marker. Make sure you can see the design on the reverse side or draw it in.

2 Use a light table or window to trace the star one quarter at a time. Tape fabric onto glass table with the light source underneath or on a window, leaving the bottom edge of the fabric untaped to ease turning to trace the complete star.

3 With an appropriate fabric marker, lightly trace the one quarter star. Flip over and align the center of the pattern to complete the design three more times.

Star of David

12" square for quilting

Directions

1 Trace star pattern (page 119) onto paper with a dark marker.

2 Use a light table or window to trace the star. Tape fabric onto a glass table with light source underneath or on a window.

3 With an appropriate fabric marker, lightly trace the star.

4 Drawing the interlocking circles can be done with paper or drawn directly on the fabric with a compass, starting behind the top of the star.

5 To make the 3" circles, open the compass to a width of 1-1/2". Place the point of the compass at the tip of the top center star point. Draw an incomplete circle, not going through the star lines. This circle should resemble a moon coming up behind a mountain peak.

6 Next, place the point of the compass on the right side arc directly in line with the starting point and draw another circle avoiding any star lines. Continue making circles in this manner all the way around the Star of David out to the edges of the background fabric.

Patterns

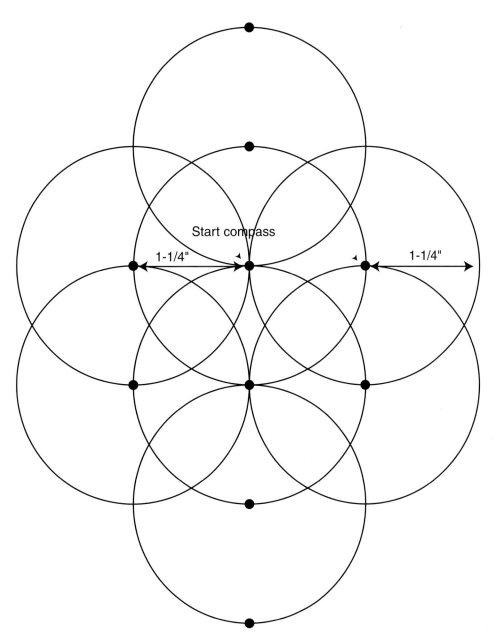

Double Wedding Ring suggested quilting motif
2-1/2" diameter intersecting circles

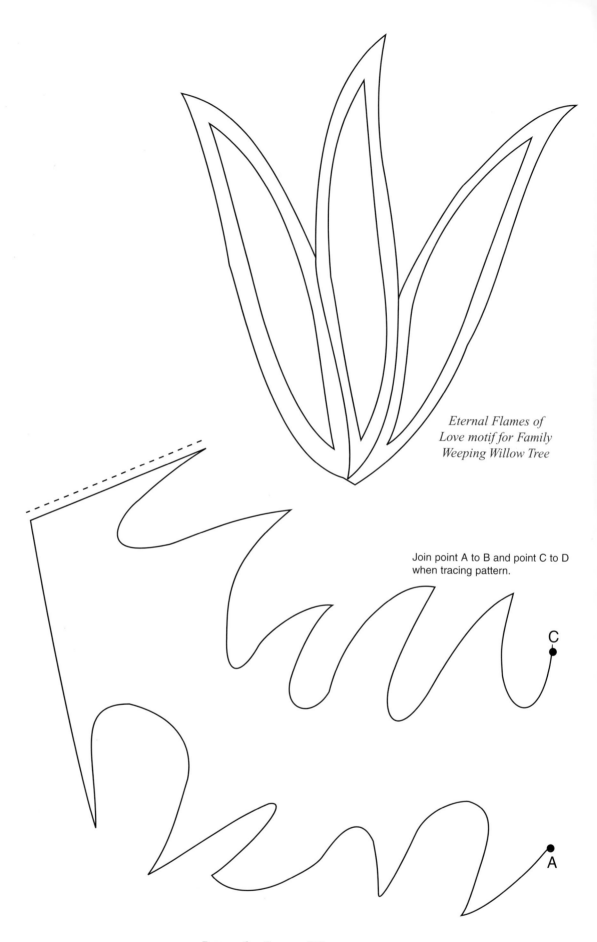

*Eternal Flames of
Love motif for Family
Weeping Willow Tree*

Join point A to B and point C to D
when tracing pattern.

C

A

Pattern for Crown of Thorns

Fold

D

B

B

C

C

C

Rose bud pattern for Family
Weeping Willow Tree

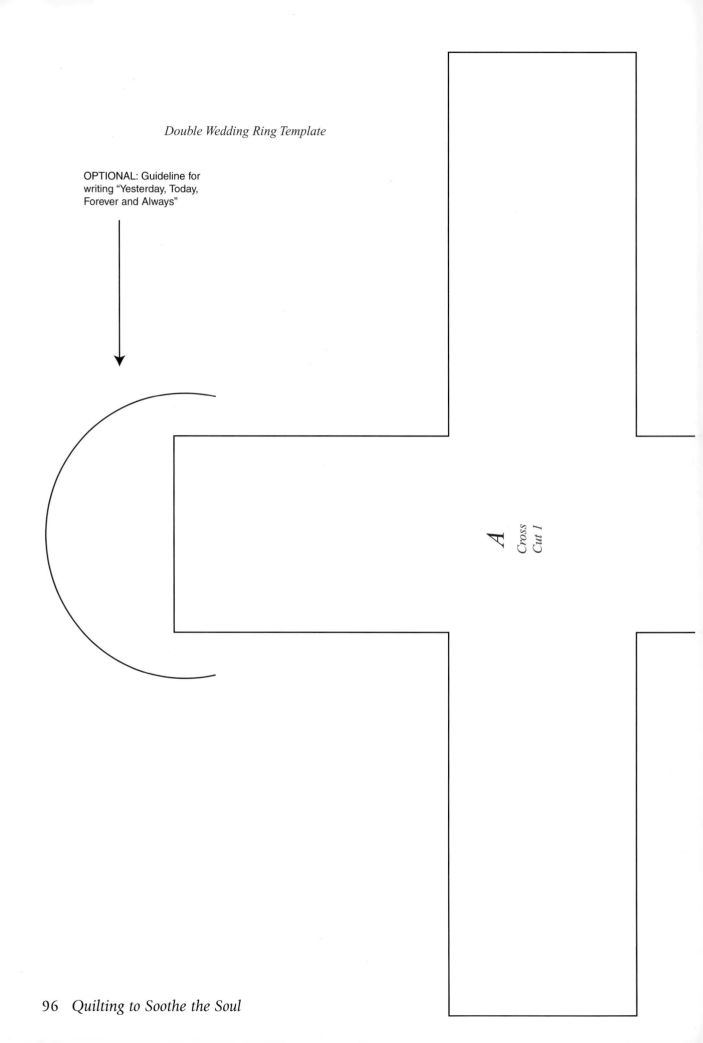

Double Wedding Ring Template

OPTIONAL: Guideline for
writing "Yesterday, Today,
Forever and Always"

A
Cross
Cut 1

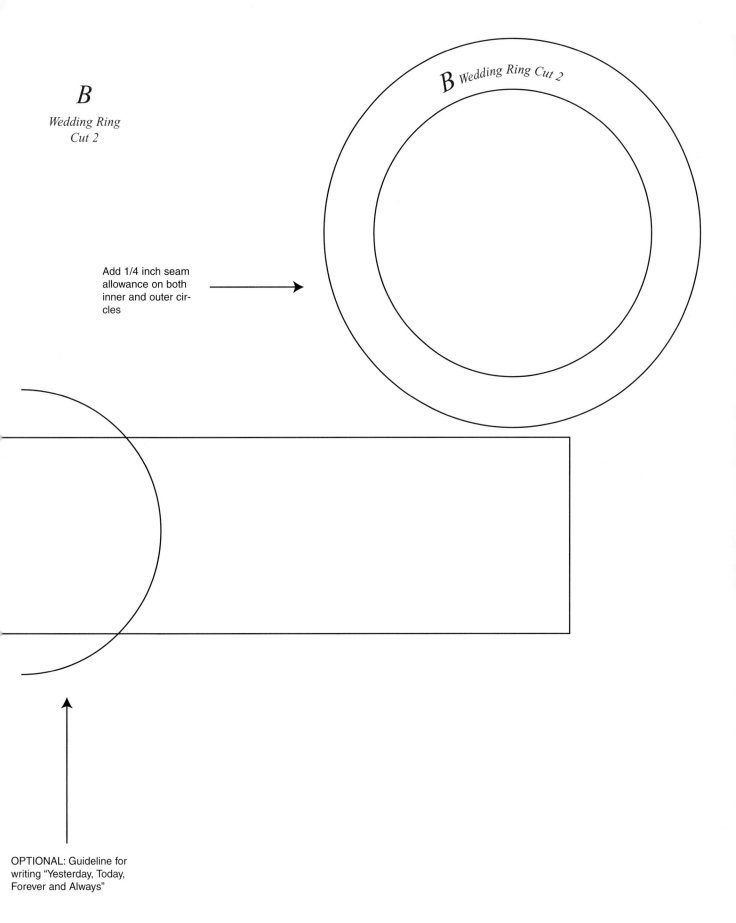

B

*Wedding Ring
Cut 2*

B Wedding Ring Cut 2

Add 1/4 inch seam
allowance on both
inner and outer cir-
cles

B Wedding Ring Cut 2

OPTIONAL: Guideline for
writing "Yesterday, Today,
Forever and Always"

Optional leaves for White Roses

Cross appliqué
Crown of Thorns

*Guiding Star quilting motif
for Family Weeping Willow Tree*

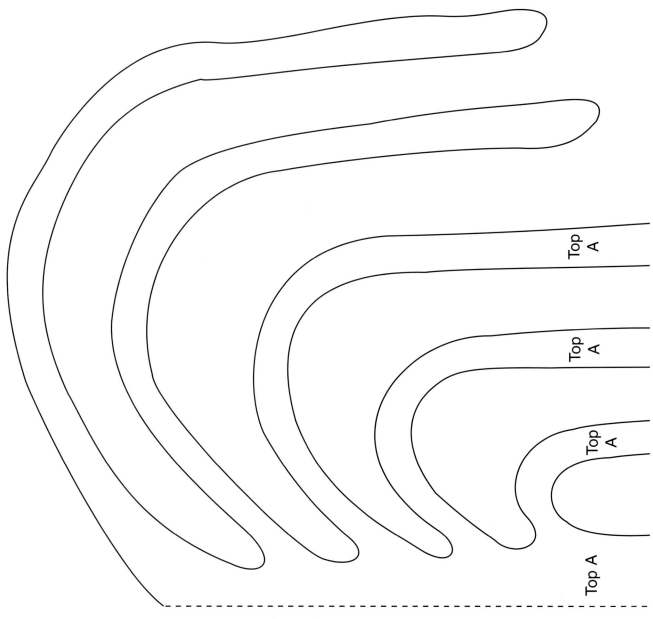

Top A

Top A

Top A

Top A

Weeping Willow appliqué for Family Weeping Willow Tree

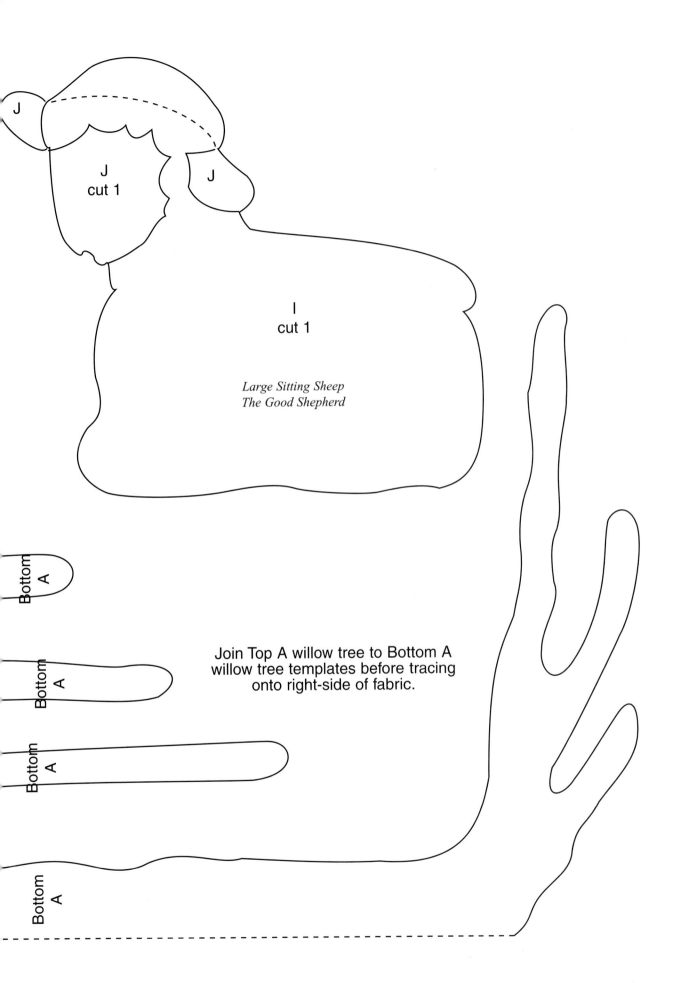

J

J
cut 1

J

I
cut 1

Large Sitting Sheep
The Good Shepherd

Bottom A

Bottom A

Bottom A

Join Top A willow tree to Bottom A
willow tree templates before tracing
onto right-side of fabric.

Bottom A

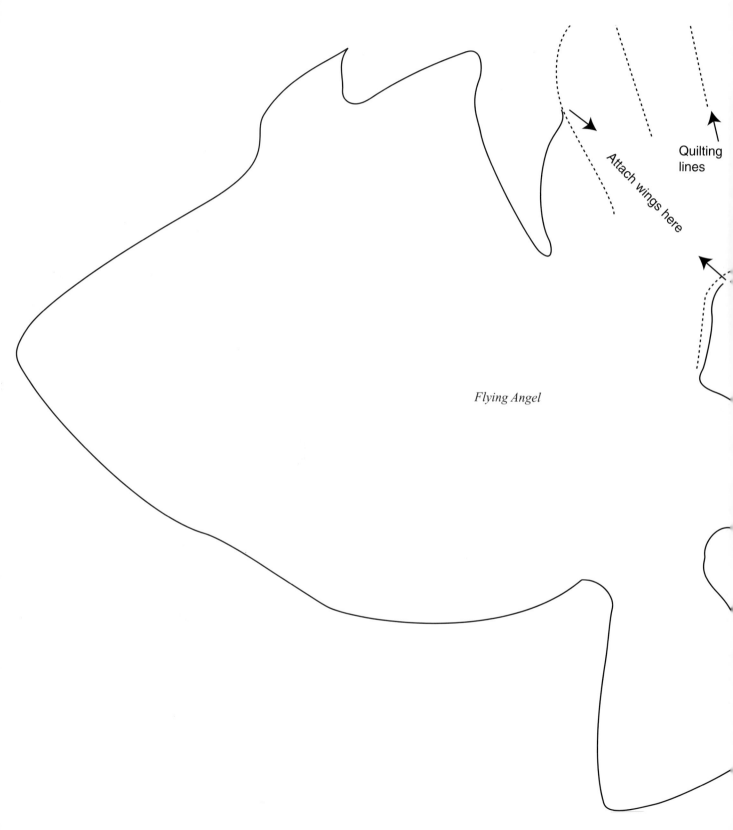

Quilting
lines

Attach wings here

Flying Angel

Quilting Motif

L
cut 1

K
cut 1

Large Standing Sheep
The Good Shepherd

M

N

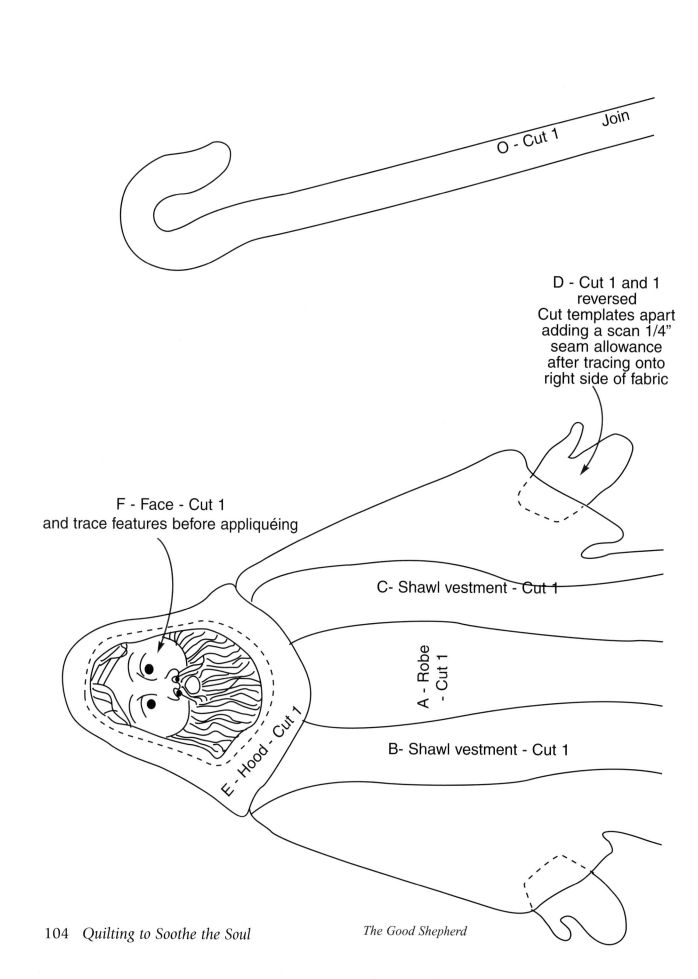

O - Cut 1   Join

D - Cut 1 and 1
reversed
Cut templates apart
adding a scan 1/4"
seam allowance
after tracing onto
right side of fabric

F - Face - Cut 1
and trace features before appliquéing

C- Shawl vestment - Cut 1

A - Robe
- Cut 1

E - Hood - Cut 1

B- Shawl vestment - Cut 1

Join O to O O - Cut 1

H

H
Cut 1

H

G
Cut 1

Lamb

Quilting Motif

Quilting
lines

Attach to angel body

Quilting Motif
7½" x 5¾"
Shown at 50%

Quilting lines

Mourning Doves

Flying Angel Quilting Motif
10½" wide x 5" long
Shown at 50%

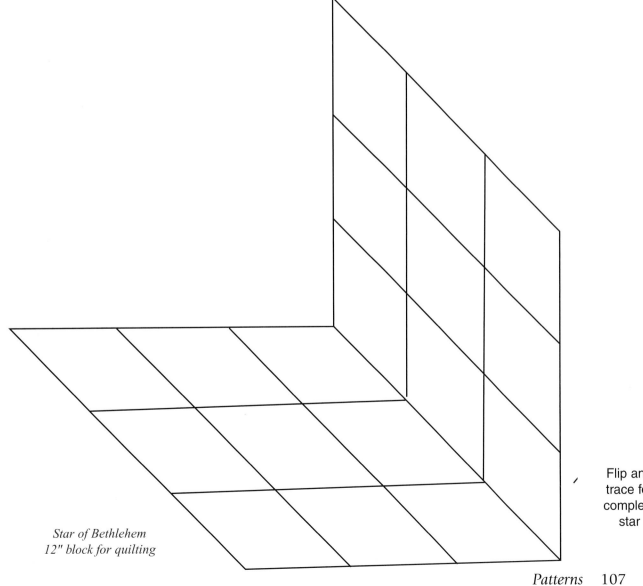

Flip and
trace for
complete
star

Star of Bethlehem
12" block for quilting

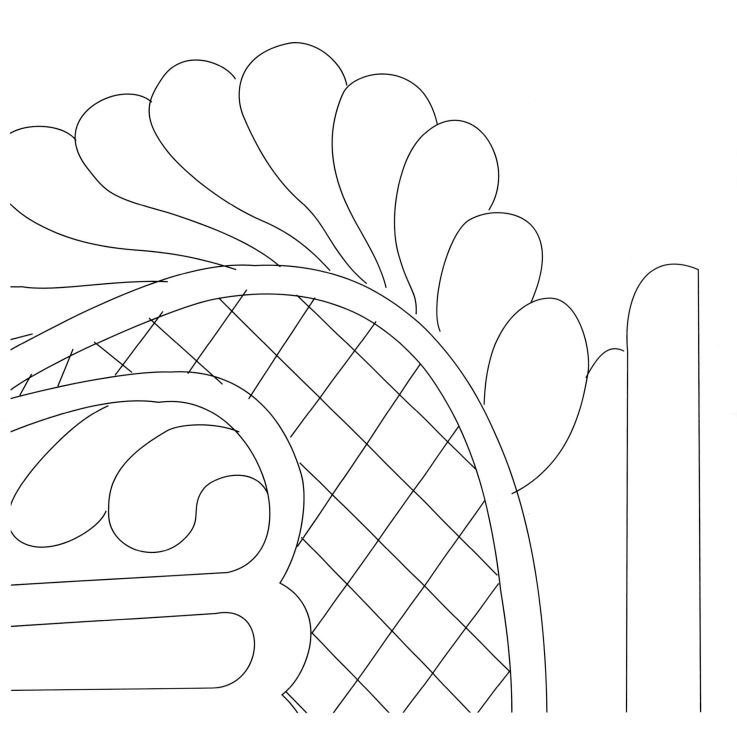

Heavenly Harp A

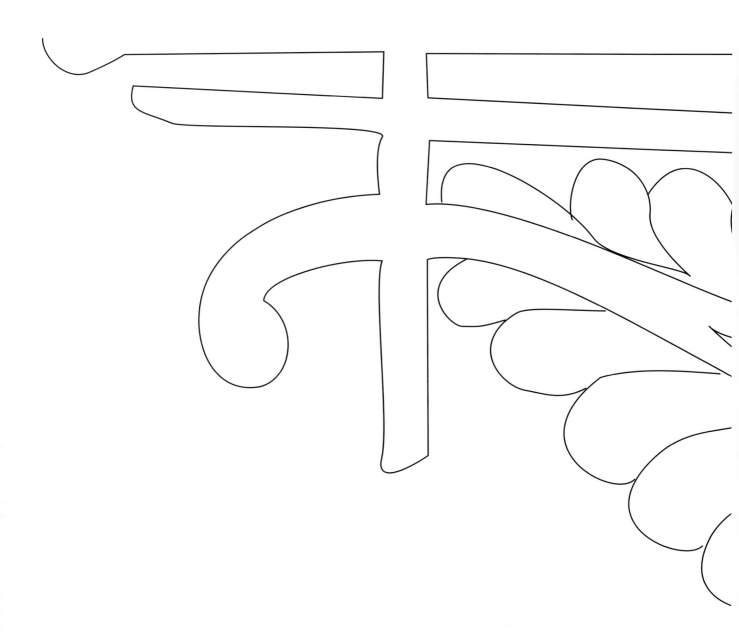

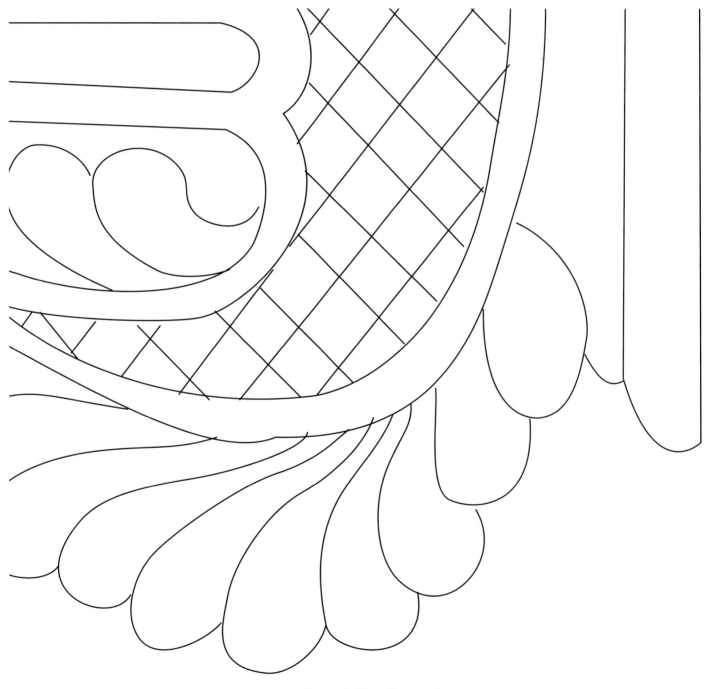

Heavenly Harp B

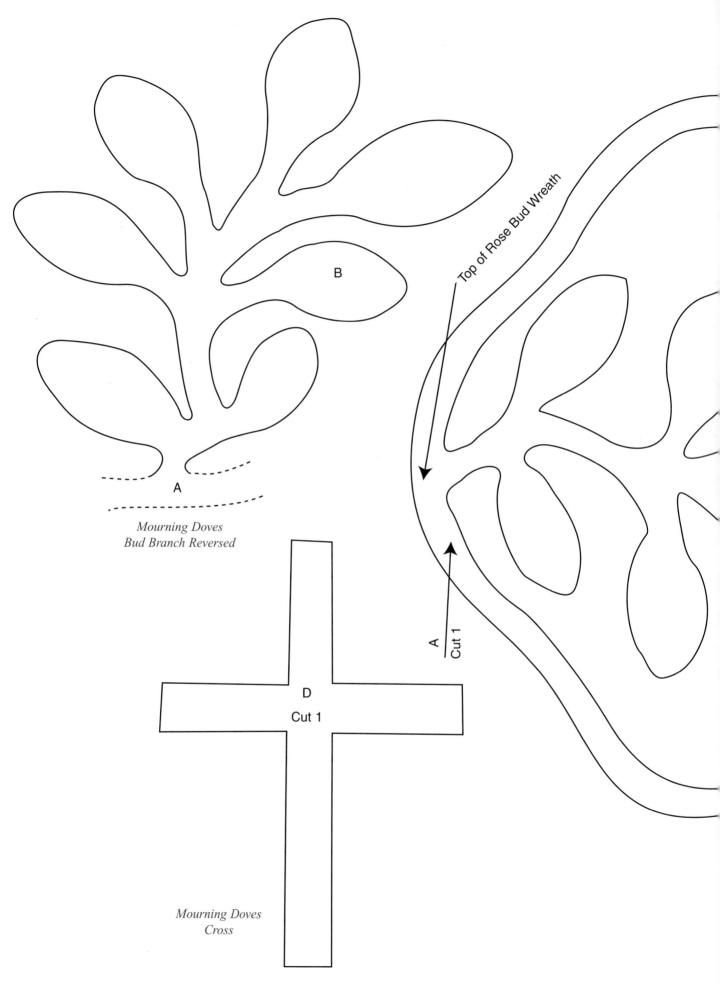

B

A

Mourning Doves
Bud Branch Reversed

Top of Rose Bud Wreath

A
Cut 1

D
Cut 1

Mourning Doves
Cross

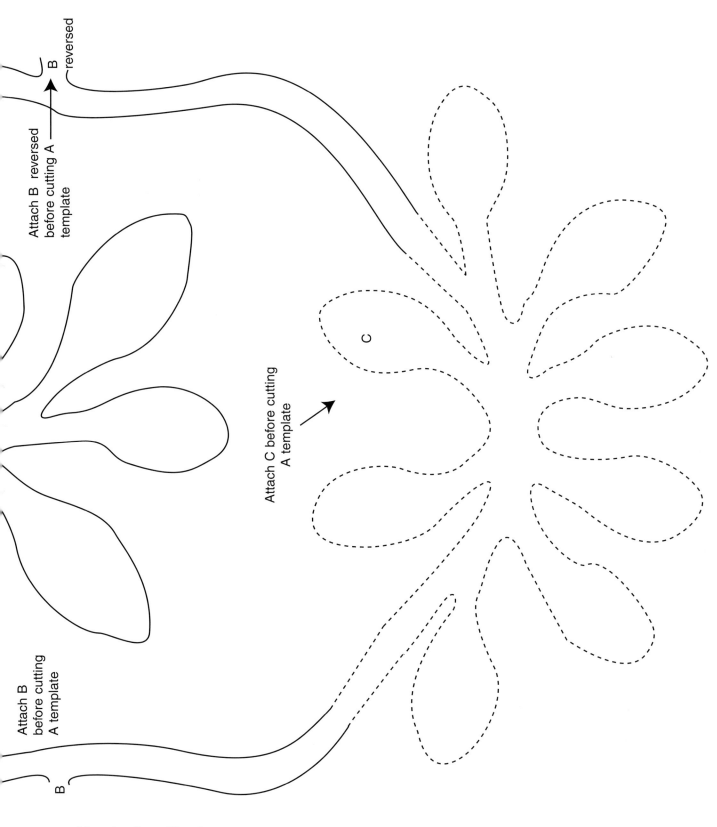

Attach B reversed
before cutting A
template

B
reversed

Attach C before cutting
A template

C

Attach B
before cutting
A template

B

Mourning Doves Wreath

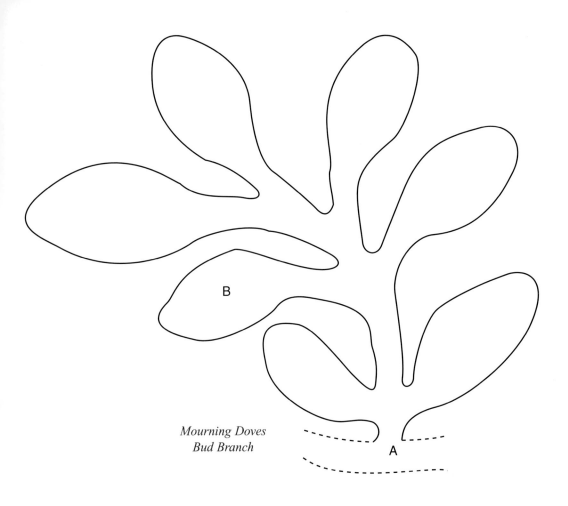

*Mourning Doves
Bud Branch*

B

A

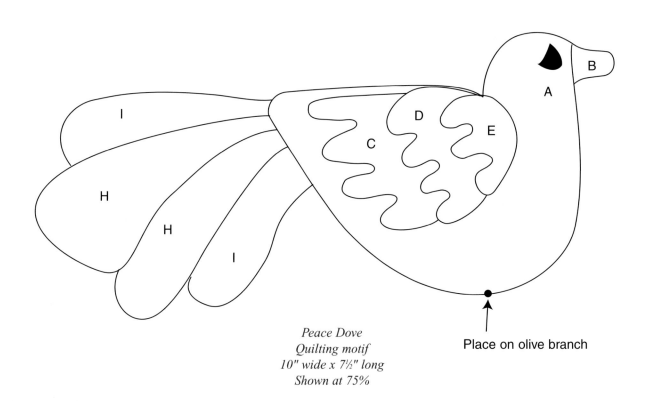

*Peace Dove
Quilting motif
10" wide x 7½" long
Shown at 75%*

Place on olive branch

B

A

D

E

C

I

H

H

I

Quilting Motif for long sides 9¼" x 4¼"
(omit bud branch under appliquéd
wreath)
Shown at 50%

Connect at dots

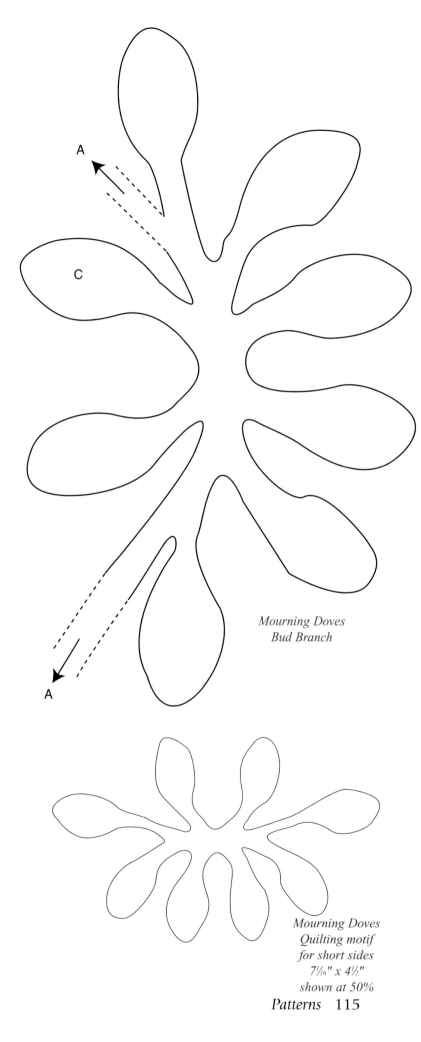

A

C

A

Mourning Doves
Bud Branch

Mourning Doves
Quilting motif
for short sides
7¹⁄₁₆" x 4½"
shown at 50%

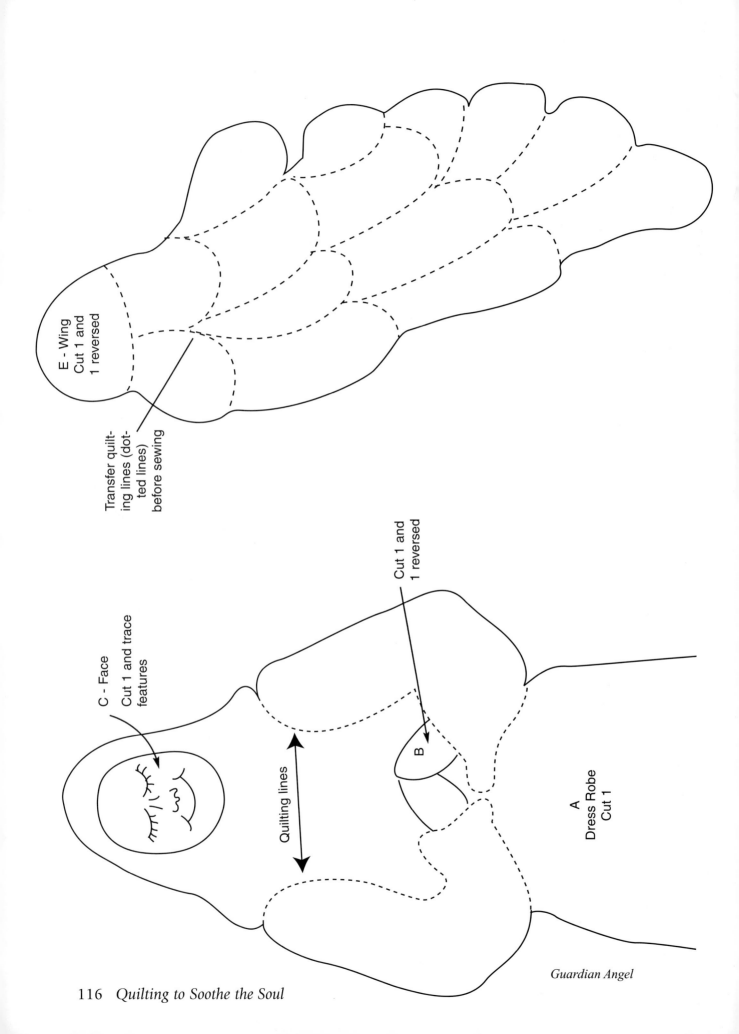

E - Wing
Cut 1 and
1 reversed

Transfer quilt-
ing lines (dot-
ted lines)
before sewing

Cut 1 and
1 reversed

C - Face
Cut 1 and trace
features

Quilting lines

B

A
Dress Robe
Cut 1

Guardian Angel

*Guardian Angel
quilting motifs*

D - Halo
Cut 1

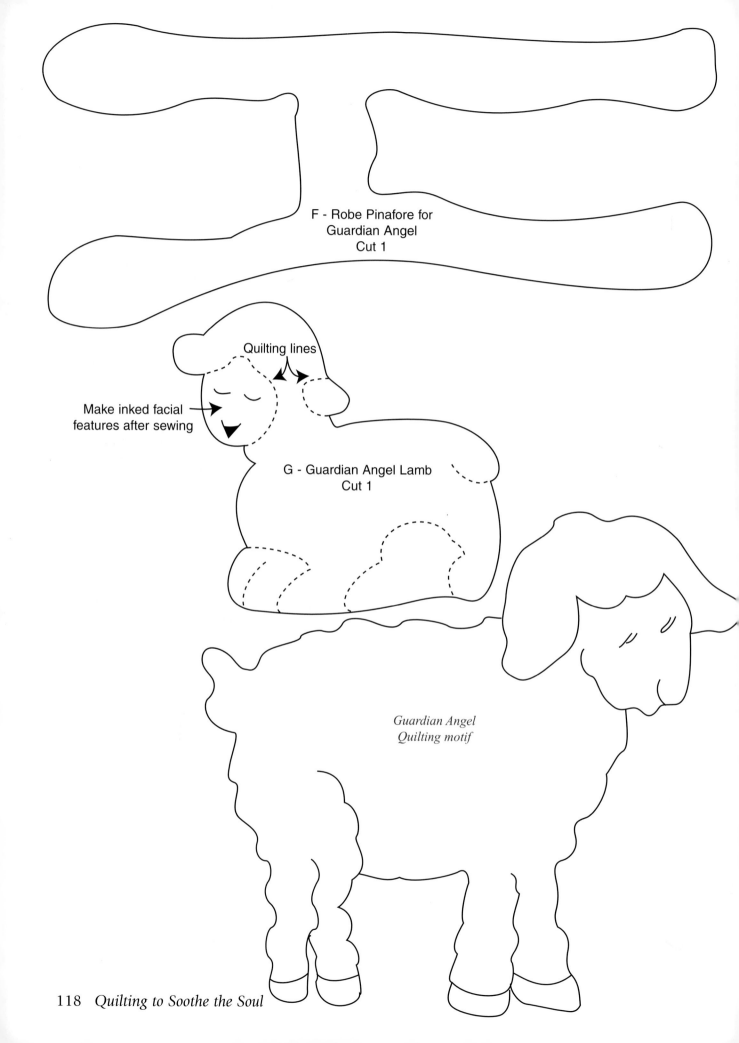

F - Robe Pinafore for
Guardian Angel
Cut 1

Quilting lines

Make inked facial
features after sewing

G - Guardian Angel Lamb
Cut 1

Guardian Angel
Quilting motif

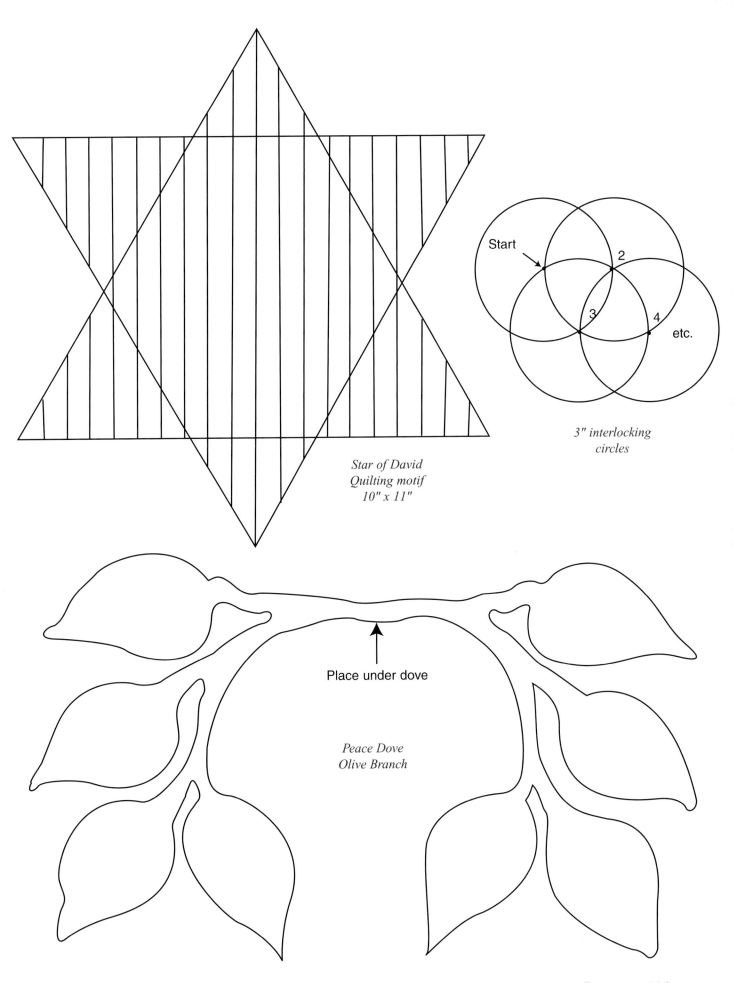

Star of David
Quilting motif
10" x 11"

Start

2

3 4 etc.

3" interlocking
circles

Place under dove

Peace Dove
Olive Branch

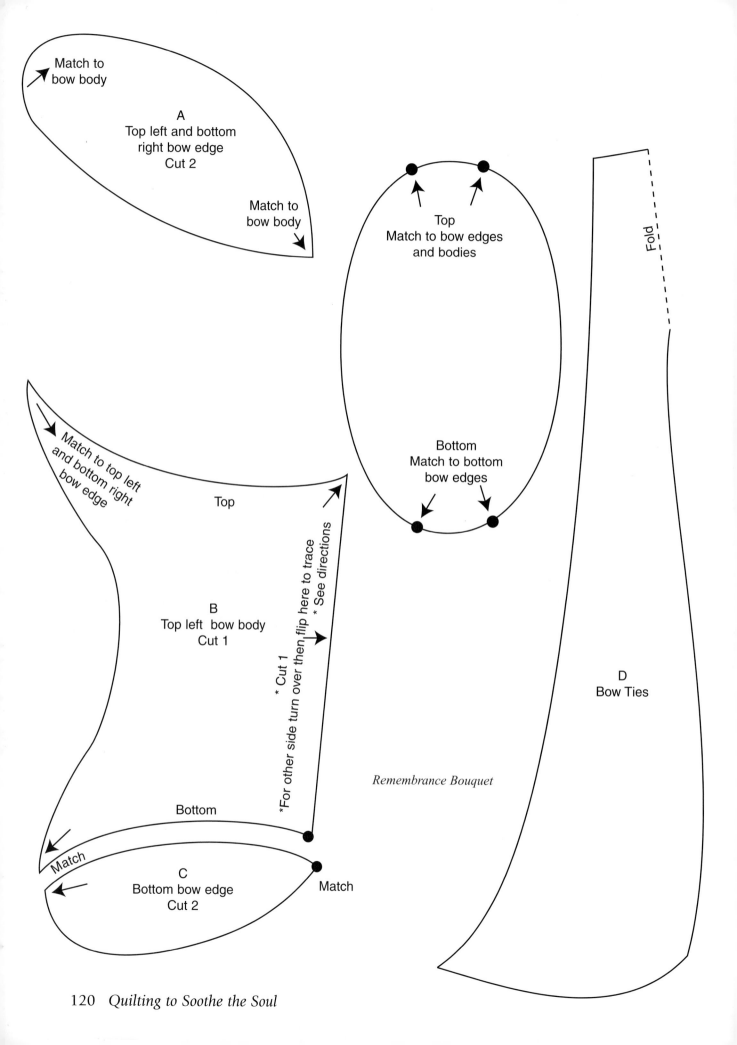

Match to
bow body

A
Top left and bottom
right bow edge
Cut 2

Match to
bow body

Top
Match to bow edges
and bodies

Bottom
Match to bottom
bow edges

Fold

Match to top left
and bottom right
bow edge

Top

B
Top left bow body
Cut 1

*For other side turn over then flip here to trace   * See directions

* Cut 1

Bottom

Match

C
Bottom bow edge
Cut 2

Match

D
Bow Ties

Remembrance Bouquet

120   *Quilting to Soothe the Soul*

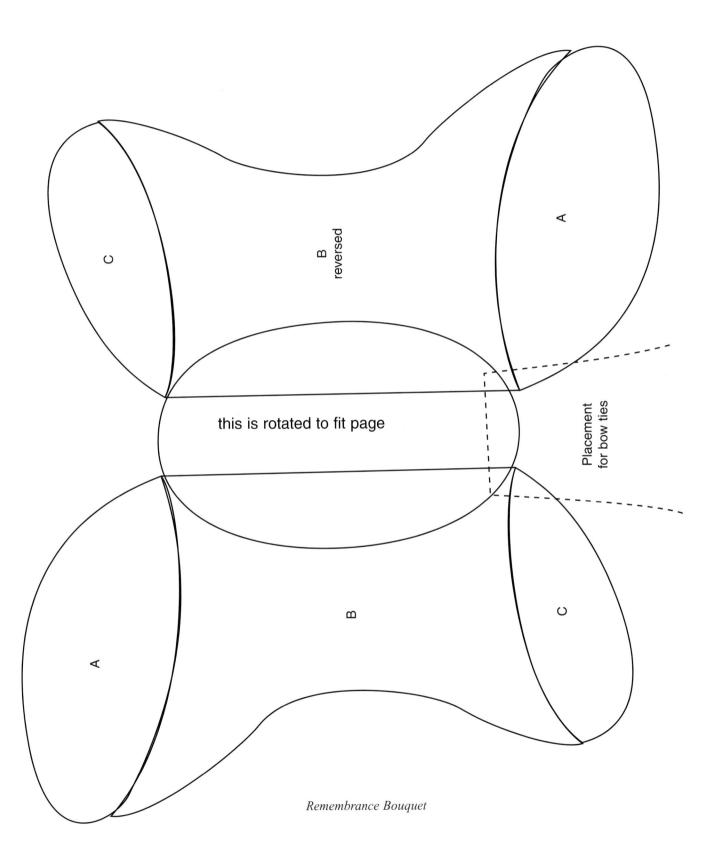

C

B
reversed

A

this is rotated to fit page

Placement
for bow ties

A

B

C

Remembrance Bouquet

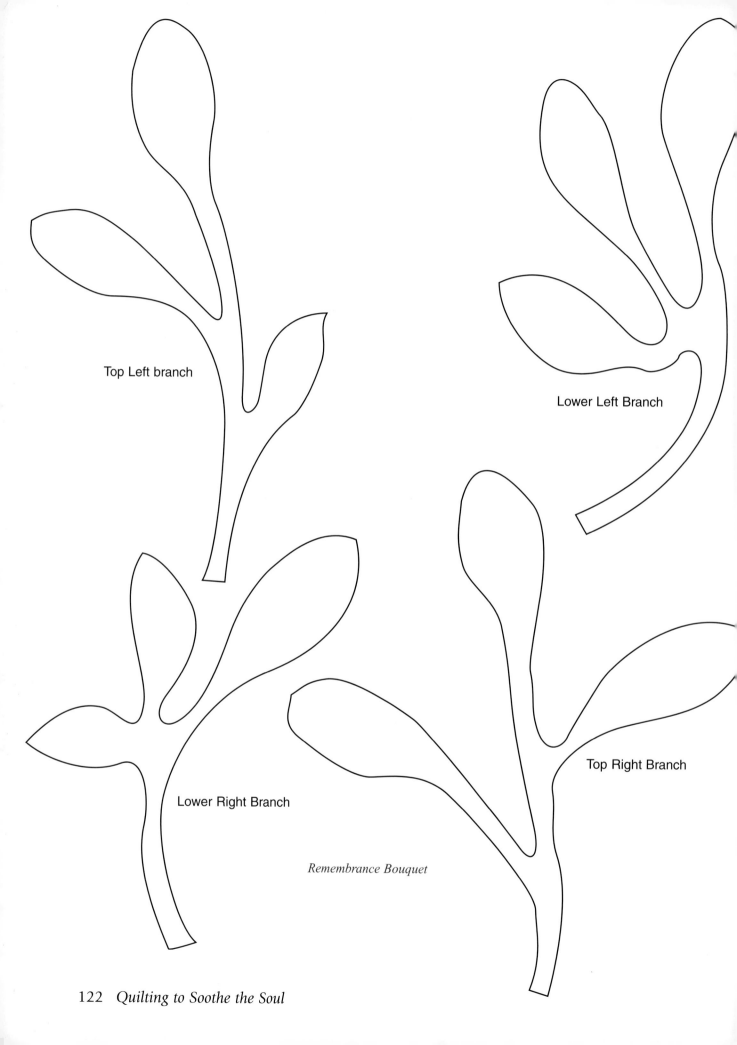

Top Left branch

Lower Left Branch

Lower Right Branch

Top Right Branch

Remembrance Bouquet

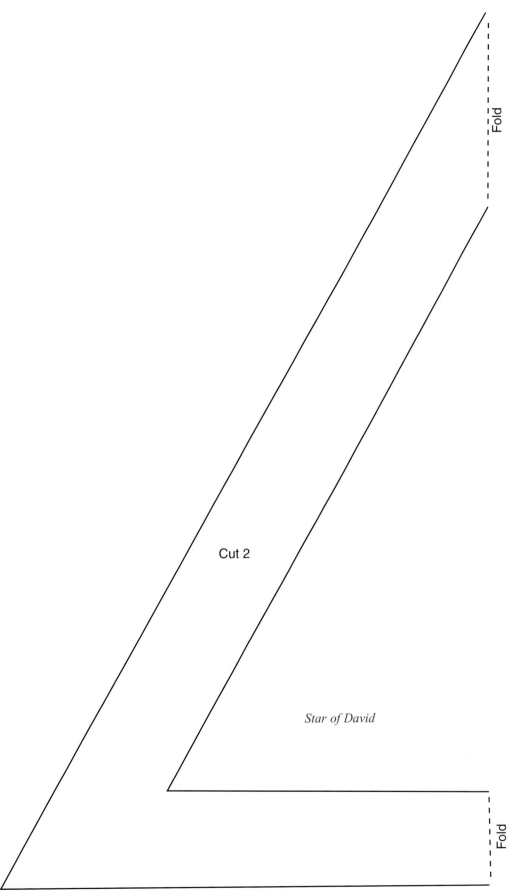

Cut 2

Star of David

Fold

Fold

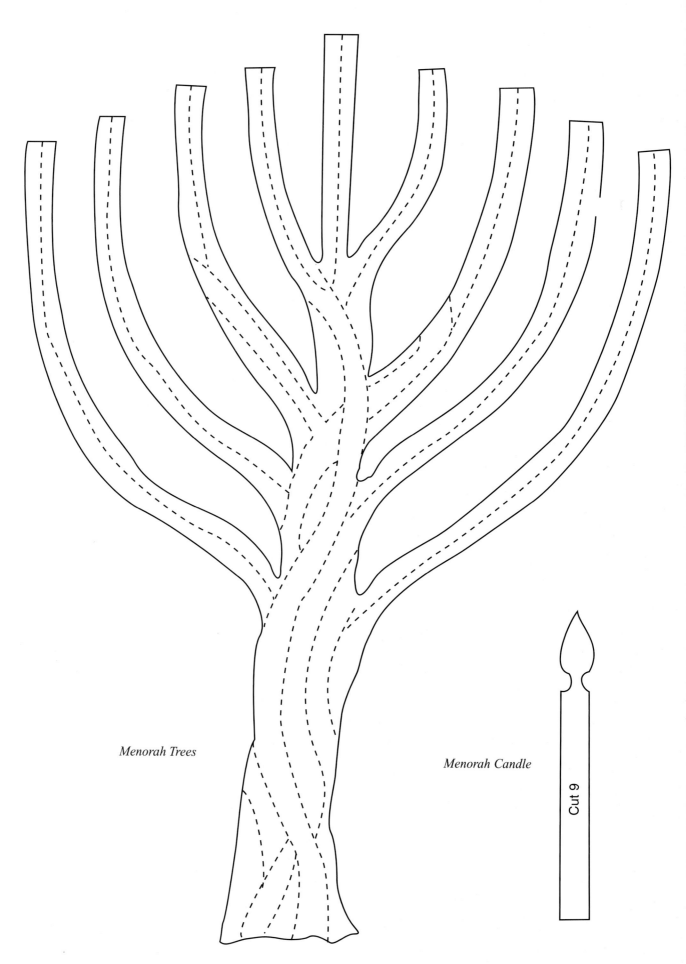

Menorah Trees

Menorah Candle

Cut 9

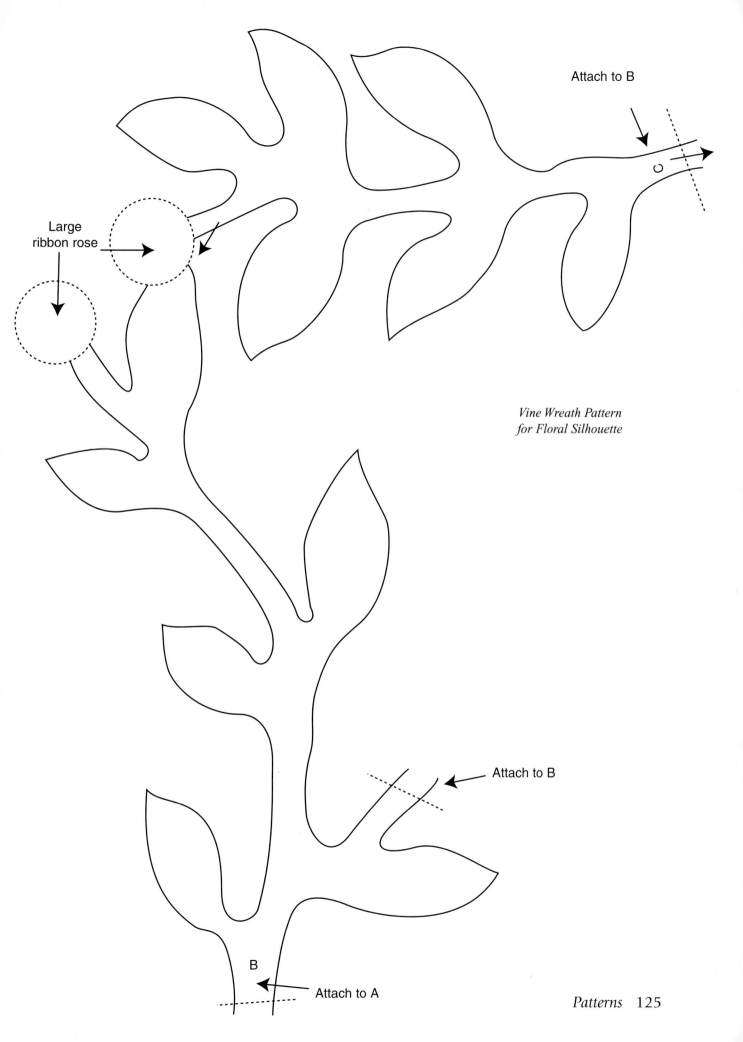

Attach to B

Large
ribbon rose

*Vine Wreath Pattern
for Floral Silhouette*

Attach to B

B

Attach to A

Patterns 125

Attach to B

A

Place on fold

Vine Wreath Pattern for Floral Silhouette,
continued

Footnotes

1 Carol Williams Gebel, *Final Rites of Passage Quilts: Quilts Wrap the Deceased for Burial and Line Coffins* (San Francisco: *Uncoverings*, 1995), 206.

2 Author's note: But in June 1999, scientists and researchers from the Hebrew University of Jerusalem found pollen grains and plant images in it that come only from an area around Jerusalem during March and April matching a traceable first century burial face cloth known as the Sudarium of Oviedo, which is believed to have covered Jesus' face. Also, both cloths have type AB blood stains in similar patterns. *Mexico Ledger*, (August 2, 1999), page 5.

3 Habenstein, Robert W. and Lamers, William M., *Funeral Customs the World Over*, 4th ed. Revised by Howard C. Raether, Milwaukee, WI: Bulfin Printers, Inc. 1994), 320.

4 *Ibid, 410.*

5 *Ibid, 444.*

6 *Ibid, 456-461.*

7 *Ibid, 466-468.*

8 *Ibid, 596.*

9 Cross Bywater Mary, *Treasures In the Trunk Quilts of the Oregon Trail* Nashville, TN: Rutledge Hill Press. 1993, 64.

10 Amelia Peck, *American Quilts & Coverlets in The Metropolitan Museum of Art* (New York, NY): The Metropolitan Museum of Art, New York, and Dutton Studio Books, New York. 1990, 98-99.

11 Gebel, 206-213.

12 Gail Andrews Trechsel, "Mourning Quilts in America" in *Uncoverings* 1989, ed. Laurel Horton (San Francisco, CA: American Quilt Study Group, 1990), 146-148.

13 *Country Living*, October 2000 Vol. 23 NO. 10, 74-76.

14 Goldthorpe, Carolyn, *From Queen to Empress, Victorian Dress 1837-1877*. New York: The Metropolitan Museum of Art, 1988. p. 73.

15 Sandi Fox, *For Purpose and Pleasure Quilting Together* (Nashville, TN: Rutledge Hill Press, 1995), 120.

16 Ibid., 120.

17 David E. Stannard, "Sex, Death and Daguerreotypes" in *America & the Daguerreotype*, ed. John Wood (Iowa City, IA: University of Iowa Press, 1991), 104.

18 Fox, 26.

19 Ibid., 63-64.

20 Ibid., 44.

21 Ibid., 48.

22 Ibid., 58.

23 *Traditional Quiltworks*, #79, 5-6.

24 Gebel, 203-210.

25 Quoted in Carol Williams Gebel, "Quilts in Native American Giveaways".. 216-218.

26 Habenstein and Lamers, 687-691.

27 Sandi Fox. "When Thou Art Gone to Western Land" 133.

28 Carol Williams Gebel, 220. (Gebel also sites several such quilts in the subsection "Quilts Made From Textiles Used in Funerals", 218-220.)

29 Carol Williams Gebel, 207.

30 Orlofsky, Patsy and Myron, *Quilts in America*, Chapter 7 "Types of Quilts," (New York: McGraw-Hill, 1974), 242-243.

31 Linda Otto Lipsett, Elizabeth Roseberry Mitchell's *Graveyard Quilt An American Pioneer Saga* (Dayton: Halstead & Meadows Publishing, 1995), 18.

32 Ibid., 20.

33 *Quilter's Newsletter Magazine*, November 1995/#277, 12.

34 Gebel, 207.

35 E. Duane Elbert and Rachel Kamm Elbert, *History From the Heart-Quilt Paths Across Illinois* (Nashville, TN: Rutledge Hill Press, 1993, 72.

36 Gebel, 201-203.

37 Gebel, 205-206.

38 Habenstein and Lamers, 762.

39 American Quilter, Winter 2000/Volume XVI, No. 4, 14.

About the author

Linda Carlson's educational background includes two bachelor's degrees: elementary education and K-12 music education from the University of Missouri at Columbia. While teaching second grade, she became certified by the Library of Congress to transcribe Braille; and there resides her transcription of Shel Silverstein's *A Light in the Attic*. These degrees and experiences prepared her for a career in quilting in that she possesses a good sense of humor, is patient, flexible yet guiding, and allows her students to follow the creative beat of their own drummer.

Since the early 1980s, Linda has taught all areas of quilting, specializing in appliqué and the history of and techniques in making the large four-block quilt in the latter part of the decade. Teaching throughout Missouri and the rest of the United States for guilds, retreats, symposiums, and large quilt shows such as the American Quilter's Society Show in Paducah, Kentucky, Quilt Odyssey in Gettysburg, Pennsylvania, and the International Quilt Festival in Houston, Texas has kept her quite busy.

For the past 10 years she has judged quilt shows, Missouri fairs and contests for Wal-Mart. "Judging quilt shows is one of the very best experiences," Linda says, "that I bring back to my students to help them improve all of their quiltmaking techniques for creating a visually pleasing and skillfully-executed quilt."

The American Quilter's Society published her first two books in 1994 and 1997 respectively: *Roots, Feathers & Blooms: Four-Block Quilts, Their History & Patterns, and Four-Blocks Continued...* . In 1995, she presented a research paper, "The Roots of the Large Four-Block Quilt" for the symposium "What's American About American Quilts?" at the Smithsonian Institution in Washington, D.C., sponsored by the American Quilt Defense Fund and the Smithsonian Institute. Later, in 1996, she received the G. Andy Runge Ambassador Award in recognition of her representation of Mexico, Missouri, during her many teaching excursions. Since then, about thirty of Linda's four-block collection of quilts were exhibited at the MAQS Museum in Paducah, Kentucky. She has written articles for several national magazines, including *Lady's Patchwork Circle, Quilter's Newsletter*, *Quilting International, Fabric Showcase Special*, and *Quilting Today*. Some of Linda's quilts, both new and antique, have been featured in books such as *A Quilted Christmas* edited by Bonnie Browning at AQS, *Quilts A Living Tradition* by Robert Shaw and Marie Salazar's book from Michael Friedman Publishing Group, Inc. Recently, Linda's articles on fabric choices and quilts and the grieving process have appeared in *Quilting Today's 1999 Fabric Special* and the 2001 Spring issue of the *American Quilter's Society Magazine*. In March 2001, Linda was a guest artist at the Elly Sienkiewicz Appliqué Academy in Williamsburg, Virginia. Linda's work has also been featured in such exhibitions as: "United We Stand," Paducah, Kentucky, 2002 American Quilter's Society Show with her quilt titled, "What So Proudly We Hailed" (currently on a two- to three-year loan); at "Remember When ...", the Paducah, Kentucky, 1997 American Quilter's Society Show invitational and touring exhibit, with her quilt titled "Remember When We Built Our Dream Home Back in 1996?" Linda also exhibited at the Museum of American Quilter's Society in Paducah, Kentucky, "Grand and Glorious: Four Block Quilts from the Collection of Linda Carlson," in 1997.

Linda's workshops and lectures offer 27 classes featuring hand appliqué and/or pieced four-block quilt projects—from large appliqué pieces to intricate *scherenschnitte* designs, with some machine projects, too; commemorative/memorial quilts; designing specific features for quilts such as feather borders, center and corner treatments; perfecting appliqué and 3-D techniques; and choosing background and quilting motifs.

"As I continue to teach around the country, I am always inspired by my students' undiscovered talents," Linda says. "I've learned so much from them, and hope I have opened their eyes to their own creativity."